SL 32

TEACHING LANGUAGES

TEACHING LANGUAGES

A Notebook of Suggestions and Recollections

BY

I. C. THIMANN B.A. B.Com. Ph.D.

CHIEF MODERN LANGUAGE MASTER NOTTINGHAM HIGH SCHOOL

GEORGE G. HARRAP & CO. LTD

LONDON TORONTO WELLINGTON SYDNEY

First published in Great Britain 1955
by GEORGE G. HARRAP & CO. LTD.
182 High Holborn, London, W.C.1

COMPOSED IN BASKERVILLE TYPE AND PRINTED AT THE PITMAN PRESS, BATH
MADE IN GREAT BRITAIN

PREFACE

THIS book is concerned solely with the teaching of modern languages. It has little or nothing to say about salaries, promotion, class discipline, rewards and punishments, the psychology of children and inspectors: and contains only those personal reminiscences which bear upon the subject.

I hope that what I write will not seem too superior. There are books on teaching whose authors are too perfect for words: do they ever admit failure? Are their pupils always enthusiastic? Is every lesson a minor triumph?

I trust, too, that these notes will be free of that distressing jargon which lies heavy on books about teaching. Perhaps Education, rather than Economics, should be called "the dismal science." Such is obviously the view of those who, at public libraries, give the Education section a wide berth. The preface of one book that I possess tells me that:

> The approach is dominated by a socio-cultural point of view rather than an eclectic one, the latter being pedagogically weak.

I have never got past this sentence.

Vague idealism also I have tried to avoid. I like to consider what might be and what ought to be, but I am concerned for the most part with what is. I cannot think that twenty years hence the lot of the language teacher is likely to be very different.

Language teaching, as I shall hope to show, suffers because its aims are ill-defined. We have never decided if we should teach languages for use, or merely as a discipline. Wavering between these objectives, we are hampered in both. But whatever our purpose, we mostly face two formidable barriers—the over-large class and the un-setted class. (There are others, such as pupils' holidays, which cannot be overcome.) At the present time, language teaching absorbs a staggering number of man-hours in day and evening schools. On the whole, I am afraid, the time is not well spent, at least by the average pupil. I should, therefore, be pleased if these notes of mine contributed in any way to greater efficiency under existing conditions, and also helped to secure smaller, better-assorted groups. The General Certificate of Education, as it develops, may assist fresh thinking. Certain aspects of it, notably the abolition of 'Ordinary' level distinctions, seem foolish and unhelpful; but, in essence, it has probably come to stay, and may even, as some of its defenders have claimed, "achieve a major educational revolution."

Lastly, I have tried, in dealing with language teaching as a whole, not to be too ambitious. One sometimes meets books with highly technical titles, such as *An ABC of Bird-watching*. In the preface its author hopes that the work will be acceptable to bird-watchers everywhere, and also to the general public. I may only hope that this book will be of some small interest to language teachers in grammar, technical, and modern schools, in technical colleges and evening institutes; to staffs of training colleges and even perhaps to teachers of other subjects. As to the general public, one's first impression is that both birds and languages leave it cold; yet, when I remember the letters provoked by past articles of mine, letters from people with a very amateur interest in foreign languages, I am not so sure. Many people have tried to learn a foreign language; some never give up trying; and nobody denies the national importance of efficiency in this field.

Incidentally, some of the ideas in this book have already been expressed in article form: on this account, I ask the indulgence of the Editors of *The Times Educational Supplement*, *The Journal of Education*, *World Review*, *Fortnightly*, *Contemporary Review*, *Gregg Magazine*, *Business Student*, *Business Teacher* and the *A.M.A. Journal*.

I. C. T.

CONTENTS

Chapter One

MOVING WITH THE TIMES

THREE types of reform will increase the value of language teaching and suit it to the modern world. The first two are mere matters of organization, requiring the good-will of examining bodies. We can practise them without extensive changes in our present organization. The last can only come about as a result of major alterations in school and university policy.

1. A WINDOW ON TO THE WORLD

The England of the future may require more workers and fewer professional men; but so long as teachers, architects, doctors and accountants continue to be needed, there will be some sort of gate through which they must pass. It therefore seems likely that for some time to come the gate will only be opened to those who possess five or six passes in the General Certificate. Certainly, those going to a university now need only two or three subjects at Ordinary Level and the others at Advanced or Scholarship Level, but the principle is unchanged. It seems sensible that a doctor or an engineer should have taken a modern language in his General Certificate. English, Mathematics, French, Science, and History (or Latin, if the more conservative of our universities are sought after) make a tolerably varied selection: though some feel that an all-round education should at least include some geography, economics, or a craft.

Most grammar school pupils, therefore, will continue

with that curious test, the General Certificate foreign language. (Stephen Leacock once said that Victor Hugo would have been unable to pass our first French examination: certainly I suspect that many educated Frenchmen of to-day would be worried by its grammatical niceties.) Yet I suggest that the school language course, in a shrinking world, should offer us more than a mere passport to the professions.

Our modern language studies should afford a clear picture of the civilizations of the Western European Powers at least. In evening classes, and secondary modern schools, where linguistic time is limited; in grammar school classes where, say, French is offered as an examination subject, and, of course, in the University French degree course, we should be chiefly interested in France —though France cannot be treated in isolation. In grammar school classes or sets where the examination is not attempted (on account of the excessive difficulty of passing under present conditions), we ought to be able to go further and couple with whatever language we are studying, say French or Spanish, notes on other European countries as well. Thus, to a much greater extent than at present, the language lesson could dispel insularity and open a window on to the world: internal and external examinations, containing appropriate questions, would then be helpful.

Smith, who is quite an ordinary fellow, will switch on his radio, hear *Les Compagnons de la Chanson*, a samba band, or a Beethoven symphony. He may, on his television, view England *v*. France at rugby, an Italian film such as *Quattro Passi fra le Nuvole*, an excerpt from *Carmen*, an Austrian travelogue, or the *Song of Norway*: he is already linked to foreign programmes. At the local theatre he might enjoy a troupe of Spanish dancers, *Rigoletto*, or a translation from Molière. In all probability he has, in his drawing-room, a sultry Van Gogh reproduction. He opens his newspaper and wonders if we shall ever settle down with the Russians. A proper language course, which I shall later set out, will help him to understand and to integrate these varied experiences.

2. NEW PRIORITIES

Those who advertise in the *Situations Wanted* columns sometimes claim a "knowledge" of five languages. How many languages do you "know"? is a question one is sometimes asked. There is no sillier query. One person who has studied German for seven years may be a fine translator, but a halting speaker. Another can understand what a foreigner says, without being able to reply adequately. A third can converse fluently on a limited vocabulary. Knowledge of a language involves speaking, reading, writing, and understanding, and, even so, one of the four may lag far behind the others. Often that will not matter. It is all a question of priorities.

In organizing language classes in schools and institutes, we ought to be clear on such priorities. Only a small proportion of those who have had training in a foreign language ever writes in that language. It is hard to imagine anyone needing to do so, unless he were one of the few who produces commercial letters or advertising material or foreign broadcast scripts. Here and there, boys and girls who have had foreign correspondents at school are keeping in touch in later life. They constitute a tiny minority. If 'languages for use' is to be our doctrine, we should lay less stress on composition and translation into the foreign tongue—the latter particularly.

A much greater number go abroad, but even they are not yet a substantial proportion. Mounting costs, notably for those remote from our southern and eastern ports, may reduce the total. Those who travel do so only once or twice, as a rule, and do not always air their languages. A party of children or adults on foreign soil will always contain a fair number of introverts, and only prolonged residence will loosen their tongues; while many a useful scholar does his foreign travel with friends or parents, and is reduced to their level of timid isolation. On the other hand, we may well need to understand the foreigner, even though we have little to say in reply. It is useful to get the gist of an announcement that the cinema is on fire, or that the through coach to Bâle is in the front of the train; action on our part, not words, is called for. Speaking the language should therefore win as high a priority as writing it; understanding will be more important than either. But a reading knowledge will be the most essential accomplishment of all.

In an important Third Programme talk, called *What's Worth Learning is Worth Learning Badly*, Sir W. Hamilton Fyfe[1] placed the scholar's knowledge of a language upon a pedestal, to which few can aspire. On the other hand, he thought that we might be satisfied if, after four to five years, our pupils could read rapidly and talk glibly, even though it be with inaccurate pronunciation. Time would even show whether a smattering of two languages could be acquired in the time we now give to one.

One cannot approve inaccurate talk and pronunciation, for education should surely teach careful habits, and the scientific pronunciation and imitation of sounds give useful practice in muscular co-ordination, and valuable training for the ear. Rapid reading as an aim, however, represents languages for use, without sacrifice of discipline: most University students, for instance, and researchers require their languages for this purpose. I shall later suggest how to organize our teaching and testing in accordance with this aim. The satisfaction obtained from

[1] Third Programme, December 18, 1949.

reading menus, advertisements, signposts, quotations on the one hand, and worthwhile texts on the other hand, is acquired relatively easily and with a minimum of discouragement. It is, of course, a passive skill and must be mixed with active ones. We need not pore over complete works, where translations exist: we do not belong to a backward country, where few translations of famous books are available. One of the most enjoyable novels I have recently come across was a translation from the Finnish; but how many Albanians would have been able to read it in their own tongue, even if they had been allowed to?

3. The Choice of a Main Language

We now come to a reform over which much vain ink has been spilled. It would represent a change in policy, to which not only schools and examining bodies must subscribe, but also the universities, local authorities and the Ministry of Education itself. I know of no one who hotly opposes it, yet it seems beyond our powers to arrange. Our education system has much in common with the Mills of God.

In 1939 some 80,673 children proceeded to the School Certificate and, of those, 75,078 offered French as their modern language, 28,508 offered Latin, 10,630 German, 1252 Spanish. Other languages, Italian and Russian, were nowhere.[1] Such slight adjustments as have since occurred have not seriously upset the French monopoly in schools, though evening school programmes, of course, quickly respond to a change in demand.

To this some would reply that, before worrying over the French monopoly, we should consider abandoning the whole thesis of language for use in England, owing to the spread of English on the Continent. We learn that English is the *lingua franca* of the sea routes and air ways:

[1] J. O. Roach, *Language Studies and International Relations* (Harrap).

that over 2,000,000 are learning English on the radio,[1] and that many European intellectuals, sportsmen, businessmen and entertainers have a working knowledge of it. As I write, civilizing influences, in the shape of the American and British armies, are no doubt hastening the process. (Too rapidly, it seems, for a Society for the Maintenance of Germanic Speech was founded in 1951 to counter the influence of the Occupation, notably via American films.) Fortunately, many decades would need to elapse before the simple Western Europeans were anglicized. In any case, whether Basic or ordinary English is the medium, the results would be curious. Mr Churchill might have rubbed his eyes on learning that, in 1940, he had offered us (in Basic) "blood, toil, eye water and face water"; and perhaps the day will come when a Spanish *aduanero* will be able to say, in Basic, that the tinned foods in the traveller's luggage are dutiable. Even normal English may go pidgin, with "Okay Joe" and "You buy my postcards?" abounding; or throw up curious combinations such as *quelle pin-up!* and *tippen Sie mich off wenn der Chief kommt*. Thus we might as well put our school house in order, without waiting for the spread of English to make it unnecessary. It is illogical to have weakened the old classical monopoly, in order to set up a new one. We realize that Latin and Greek are of limited value for the majority, that they give no better training and no more 'transfer value' than French and German. We are even ceasing to teach modern languages as the classics were once taught. But we are not yet fitting language teaching to the twentieth century.

A case can be made out for French as the chief foreign language on geographical grounds; for commercial and diplomatic reasons are less valid than they were. (Inciden-

[1] *News Chronicle*, September 14, 1951 (I. Bevan, *A Lesson for Millions*).

tally, French, which is a model of precision, might seem unsuited to diplomacy, where ambiguity is often so desirable.) For a long time to come, more of our children, students, teachers and adults will have more to do with French-speaking areas (France, Belgium, Western Switzerland) than anywhere else. But that does not justify the exaggerated loyalty to French, which is, in any case, as Sir Bernard Pares has said, "the language an Englishman is least likely to speak well."[1]

Next in order I would still place German, for commercial and geographical reasons, but particularly because Anglo-German friendship is so desirable. It is essential to satisfy the German hunger for contacts in this country. Then, too, the ease of spelling and pronunciation and the virility of German have a special appeal for boys, who sometimes think that French, well spoken, sounds effeminate.

Next I would put Spanish, largely for commercial and perhaps diplomatic reasons—it is spoken by over a hundred million people. Already more people use it than French. Professor Allison Peers, in his *New Tongues*, has put the case for Spanish so eloquently that I need not stress the point. Dutch for geographical, Italian for political reasons—these would be our next priorities. There should be a limited place for Russian and the Scandinavian languages in schools. Flemish, because of its similarity to Dutch and the wide diffusion of French in Belgium, I would reject; as also Portuguese, despite the importance of Brazil. Speakers of Spanish will readily accommodate themselves to it. In further education and in the universities, of course, students can secure their own options.

It is sometimes insisted that cultural reasons should affect priorities. This is to lose sight of the fact that few

---

[1] *Journal of Education*, March 1943.

English schoolchildren will read Voltaire, Dostoïevsky or Dante in the original, flock to museums, concert halls, churches and art galleries in Lisbon and Amsterdam, or read scientific papers in the original. Furthermore, if modern studies are to provide, for the bulk of British learners, information on present-day Europe generally, it will be possible to provide an integrated view of the life, leisure and culture of a number of countries; and this, in my opinion, will be more widely useful than a knowledge of the culture of one only. The difficulty of a language is, in any case, a more pressing factor than the importance of the culture to which that language provides a passport, and that would seriously limit the scope of, say, Russian, which is, however, well suited to become a second language for gifted linguists. (I realize that Latin is often extolled because of its difficulty, but we are talking of living languages.) This factor, as we have seen, also deserves to lessen the importance of French. On the whole, cultural reasons for learning languages are uncertain and academic. The impact of Italian life, for example (via music, art, films, politics and sport), on our own is said to be considerable. Yet my *Radio Times*, for instance, with its German composers, its plays by modern French and older Russian authors, its Latin-American music, its televised Italian film, distributes its favours impartially; as does my newspaper.

To open up our language world will certainly require some long-term planning between Ministry of Education, universities, training colleges, Local Education Authorities and public schools. The position would be affected in each area by the views of the Chamber of Commerce, which would give strong commercial reasons for, say, adopting Spanish as first or second foreign language. Such planning is liable to be affected by external changes —notably currency devaluations or concessions: everyone remembers, for instance, the increased popularity of pre-war Germany at the time of the 'frozen' Mark. As I write, Austria (which has devalued) is indirectly boosting the study of German, while Switzerland (which has not) is limiting the demand for French, though its region where first-class French is spoken has never been a large one. Political changes also affect the picture—witness the post-war enthusiasm for Russian, weakened by hostility and isolation, stimulated later by the possibility of war and jobs for interpreters. But we must leave Further Education to cope with sudden fluctuations in demand.

In France, English, German, Italian, Spanish, Russian, and Arabic are all taught in *lycées* according to potential need. Why should our system remain so rigid?

Chapter Two

EARLY DAYS

I HAVE suggested that language studies should be adapted to the shrunken world of the twentieth century. This can be attempted even within the present framework; it will be made easier when the General Certificate of Education, correctly interpreted by schools and examining bodies, frees more pupils from Ordinary Level papers of the traditional kind. If classes become smaller and more homogeneous, and the quality of teachers suffers no decline, the results will be more satisfactory still.

Let us first see how our principles can be applied to the first year of the course—any course involving a class of five to forty (let us hope that this latter figure is rarely attained), and lasting four, five, six or seven years. Points applying specially to secondary modern schools and evening institutes are dealt with in special chapters.

1. USE OF THE LANGUAGE

Everyone has heard of the keen but unpunctual teacher of French who used to bid his pupils a breezy *Bonjour* on entering the classroom. Addicted to the Direct or Reform method, he waited some weeks before asking what the word meant: and none could tell him, until someone suggested 'Sorry I'm late.'

The manner of teaching a language is the first consideration, whether we are addressing eleven-year olds in grammar or modern schools, or adult classes. And if understanding a language is to be a high priority, the teacher should use it as much as possible. Yet he will not be so wedded to direct methods that he fails to translate, where necessary, a word or phrase. Use of the language stimulates mental activity; and even the least able pupils will get satisfaction from their ability to understand. Occasional lapses into English will supply variety, but its excessive use is simply an encroachment on limited time. As time passes, the use of the foreign language over increasingly longer periods can become compulsory: and a disc, hanging from the blackboard, will show when such periods are on.

A baby learns its own language by constant use of words relating to its experiences: all others it will tend to reject. Similarly, we shall build up a stock of phrases based on everyday happenings, and not on hypothetical circumstances such as are often found in phrase-books—*e.g.*, 'When I see my cousin, I shall borrow his bicycle,' or 'I have just scalded my foot.' (It is hard to see how the latter could be required in a well-organized class—unless, of course, the central heating system was faulty.)

I keep a small ancillary blackboard on which I write down phrases as they occur. The class copies them into a special section of their notebooks. This is the type of thing that is required in the first few weeks—my remarks and theirs being noted on separate pages:

French	*German*
Ferme la porte!	*Öffnet die Hefte für Grammatik!*
Ouvre les fenêtres!	
Essuie le tableau noir!	*Schliesst die Bücher!*
Est-ce que (Ramsbotham) est là? (Oui, le voilà!)	*Wechselt, bitte!*
	Wie sagt man pen auf Deutsch?
Viens me voir après la leçon!	*Komm her!*
Echangez vos copies.	*Wieviel Uhr ist es?*
Allez-vous-en!	*Was ist dir los?*
Puis-je remplir ma plume?	*Darf ich ein Stück Papier haben?*
Puis-je tailler mon crayon?	
Je ne vois pas le tableau noir.	*Hat jemand Tinte?*
	Ich verstehe nicht.

As the course progresses, this practice can be extended to include many useful words, idioms, and expressions illustrating points of grammar and syntax. For instance, pupils can be described rather than named (though the use of foreign Christian names is useful):

l'élève aux yeux bleus	Illustrating the descriptive **à** (*French*)
le garçon solide	Illustrating adjective positions (*French*)
l'élève le plus intelligent de la classe	Illustrating superlatives (*French*)
la fillette dont le père est pompier	Illustrating the omission of **un** with professions, + *dont* (*French*)
der Schüler, der eine Brille trägt	Illustrating the relative clauses (*German*)
der rothaarige Jackson	Illustrating compound adjectives (*German*)
el joven más estúpido de la clase	Illustrating superlatives (*Spanish*)

2. ACCURACY IN PRONUNCIATION

On the use of Phonetics it is a case of *Quot homines, tot sententiæ*. This is all right, provided that the members of a given staff think similarly. We shall never, of course, have large numbers of pupils who pronounce properly until:

- (*a*) classes are smaller;
- (*b*) future teachers in their degree courses are obliged by all universities to spend some months abroad;
- (*c*) modern language teachers are 'assisted' to go abroad at fairly regular intervals;
- (*d*) schools stop putting on their History or English specialists to take first-year language classes: the bad accent of the first-year teacher provides a handicap that is never properly overcome.

Yet if initial care is taken, much future irritation will be saved; for instance, oral work will flow more freely, without constant need for correction; dictations, often featuring items such as *je marché*, will be robbed of their terror; absurd pairings, such as *met* and 'met' will be avoided. Boys, as we have said, may think it effeminate to pronounce French well; but the saving of future labour will surely compensate them.

I favour the limited use of phonetic symbols, at least in French. Imitated pronunciation will do in Spanish and German, though we do not want to see printed horrors such as *pay-re-o-de-ko* and *hoy-zer*. Besides, students of the latter two languages are often proved linguists. The differences between French and English vowels are wider, and therefore need the help of science. This is forthcoming through the usual design of the mouth, showing the exact tongue and lip positions for each vowel. Pictures can also be secured, showing the lip positions from the front.

When, by such methods, the class has learned to pronounce every vowel, and especially **e**, **y**, **φ**, **œ** (single sounds, and not diphthongs), short dictations can be given (using consonants without a special phonetic symbol— *i.e.*, avoiding **ʃ**, **ʒ**, **ŋ**, and the rest). The whole process will take at least three weeks, relieved by competitions in oral and written accuracy, between two halves of a class or teams of one sort and another. Then Chapter I of the course will be started, the class, individually or in groups, reading out each section after the teacher. From now on, the phonetic symbols are used merely as a check, though pronunciation exercises will be maintained for as long as is essential. Those who constantly deviate from the norm can be told how English would sound when pronounced by a Frenchman.

Phonetic script is now no longer necessary. It seems

to many to represent a language in itself; and mediocre children may henceforward tend to write, for example, *du* as **dy** in ordinary script.

The necessary transition to ordinary script may be easily achieved, in French, by giving a key which will be added to as time goes on. An early key to help with **ɛ** and **e** would be:

Sound	Writing
ɛ	-ais -è
	-ait -ê
	-aient -et
e	-é -ez
	-er

The rolled *r* will do at the outset. I find that pupils of fourteen or fifteen suddenly begin to master the uvular *r*, and that there is little point in insisting on it at an earlier stage.

After the first three weeks, pronunciation exercises would occupy, say, the first two minutes of each lesson. Very soon the accent of the majority will be distinctly pleasant to listen to; and, strangely enough, those who are indifferent at written French are often among the neatest talkers. On the other hand, as the first year wears on, it may be found that a few can only manage an approximate pronunciation, notably of words such as *été* and *leur*, while their speech will be thick with diphthongs, as in *beau* and *tout*. To encourage this 'hard core' to talk, I would let them go, from time to time, uncorrected.

Even if intonation is not fully explained at this level, the instructor's voice must be free of monotony; but he can at any time place the familiar sound patterns on the board for the guidance of his class.

Liaison, too, should be briefly explained at this stage.

Insistence on accurate pronunciation is of great value for other subjects and techniques far removed from foreign languages—notably singing, and correct English speech. In general, a teacher who himself speaks well, and knows how to impart information, cannot afford to leave a wide gap between class pronunciation and his own. If he does, the whole question will quickly seem unimportant.

3. SPELLING IN THE FOREIGN LANGUAGE

To use the English names of letters, when it is desired to practise the foreign language as much as possible, is illogical. One sometimes sees on the blackboard, when a teacher has finished his lesson, mongrel phrases such as "*Dictée* Corrections," "*Aufsatz* for Friday"—yet these are no worse than the encroachment of English spelling on a purely French or German lesson. If phonetics are being studied, however, the use of the foreign alphabet should be deferred until the phonetic alphabet is largely done with. How confusing, for example, to record phonetically the vowel of *est* as ε and to spell it as ə ! When the names of foreign letters have been mastered, spelling tests can be given during the study of each chapter. The teacher will soon acquire a good list of problem words (*schlecht, Haupstadt, beaucoup, intéressante,* etc.) as a result of several weeks' correction.

4. LOCAL COLOUR

The aim of stimulating interest in the foreign country cannot be served too early, and I have found the following procedures useful in the teaching of French:

(i) *Wall Pictures*

Views, such as those obtainable from the London offices of foreign railways, are useless unless they are really representative, and are frequently changed. A poster depicting Mont-Saint-Michel, left hanging for a year, is in time no more distinctive than a window or a radiator.

More informative and more stimulating are annotated cuttings from an illustrated weekly. Unusual words in the captions can be underlined and their English equivalent written at the top or at the side; while a summary in bold lettering, can be inserted at the foot. One or two weekly pictures from *Point de Vue*, posted during a term, afforded us the following French characteristics:

(*a*) Virility, no less marked than among the English, via cycling, speleology, exploration (in Africa, Brazil, Greenland, etc.), swimming, basketball, scouting, underwater fishing, etc.

(*b*) Cult of the individual and relative lack of enthusiasm for team games (smallness of crowds at cup-ties, even in large urban centres, and notably at internationals).

(*c*) Past and present military and naval glories (troops in Korea and Indo-China, new aircraft-carrier).

(*d*) Natural warmth of temperament, pride in hospitality.

(*e*) Technical excellence (hydro-electric power stations, underground roads, etc.)

(*f*) Interest in Royalty.

(*g*) Economic difficulties, leading to emigration. Urban overcrowding.

Such pictures can do, and did, much to correct misapprehensions. In the early stages it is best to use foreign magazines in this way; they are usually too hard, and occasionally a little lurid, for private reading.

(ii) *Scrap Book*

A smaller group studying German has compiled a scrap-book. The *Frankfurter Illustrierte*, a passable weekly, is subscribed to; I mark pictures and captions throwing light on present-day life and characteristics, and these are pasted into the book, and a translation is appended before the book is circulated. Each member of the group is responsible for a period of one, two, or three weeks (according to his reliability).

I must add that in some Continental boarding-schools I have seen some very effective extensions of this idea, notably relief maps of England in Plasticine, wall pictures of London with cardboard models attached, etc.

We shall return to the scrap-book especially (page 88), and to local colour in general, in later chapters.

5. The Language Course

(i) *Ideal Books*

We are now ready to begin the first-year course. Books are open at page one. It is to be hoped that they are cheerful and nearly new, not too prosy, nor dog-eared; with sensible pictures, not of desks and blackboards, but of foreign places and people (French boys in many pre-war primers were particularly weedy and effeminate); well-spaced print; vocabulary set out before each chapter, preferably according to parts of speech; and plenty of heavy type for the salient points. We ought to plunge straight into the foreign scene after some introductory talks in English about the foreign country—talks at first hand, for preference, though English teachers, I think, are less enterprising over foreign travel than their Continental counterparts.

If, say, Germany is the theme, there should be a distinct narrative element—a German family in familiar surroundings, or an English visitor touring the Reich.

Other requirements for the ideal book are: grammar set down as it occurs, preferably after each chapter, and not relegated, in an indigestible mass, to the end of the book; exercises, not too few and not too many, cunningly testing past work with present.

(ii) *Pattern of a Lesson*

This, I suggest, is the way to treat the reading matter:

(*a*) Reading, sentence by sentence, by the teacher (not forgetting intonation).

(*b*) Repetition by class (*en masse*, in groups, or individually).

(*c*) Grammar, contributed by the class as a result of the reading (or explained by the instructor before the reading), and written down in special note-books. For anything at all difficult or technical, English may be used; and, at that, it may be necessary to explain what adverbs, conjunctions, etc., are (page 33).

(*d*) Vocabulary, written down in columns, and attaching especially the article:

French	*English*
le toit	the roof
puisque	since

German	*English*
der Wind	the wind
fallen	to fall

In German, it may be well to add noun plurals, even though none emerge during the first few chapters—useful advance information, this. Similarly, the irregular 2nd and 3rd person singular of the present tense should be spoken of, and noted thus:

der Wind (-e)	the wind
fallen (ä)	to fall

In due course the full gamut of irregularities of the strong verbs will fall to be noted; so will the separable or inseparable nature of the verb, not to mention an asterisk for verbs taking *sein*:

arbeiten	to work
*eilen	to hurry
*fallen (ä, ie, a)	to fall
*ein-steigen (ie, ie)	to climb in
vergessen (i, a, e)	to forget

It may be objected that, under the doctrines of "languages for use," we should look on undue use of English as a waste of time, and use definitions instead of equivalents, thus helping the individual to think in the foreign language:

le déjeuner	*le second repas du jour*
der Hügel	*ein kleiner Berg*
la primavera	*la primera estación*

Drawings too will certainly help us to avoid English; an extract from an early Spanish notebook would record:

la mesa

la silla

el pupitre

On the whole, though, these procedures are too cumbersome at this stage, save with very simple definitions and designs. (Avoid trying to define *puisque*, *denn*, *porque!*) But the definition, rather than the equivalent, is very desirable in later stages, even though certain obstinate learners will always translate to themselves, evolving a mental process like this:

le déjeuner—*le second repas*—the second meal—lunch

Thus, it is doubtful if we can avoid the mental coupling of *déjeuner* with 'lunch.' Duller children are confused by definitions, and even the brighter ones will be making a mental translation. Later, we can incorporate *déjeuner* into the oral lesson, getting relatively rapid answers to such questions as *A quelle heure est le déjeuner?*

(*e*) Translation of obscure passages, if any.

(*f*) Re-reading, with comprehension questions in the foreign language (notice of questions being given to slower pupils); and finally, grammar questions. The comprehension questions, normally set down in the book, may be added to by any of the learners; if the latter are materialistic, or thrive in a competitive atmosphere, sides may be chosen (*Butlin, tu es le capitaine: je choisis Oscroft; un point pour l'équipe de Betty*, etc.) and questions bandied about from team to team. Further translation from English can now be dispensed with.

(*g*) Reproduction essays, both oral and written, based on short plans given on the blackboard.

(*h*) Dictation. After the first seven processes have been completed, success in the dictation should be assured; but more backward groups should be given an opportunity to prepare the piece, at any rate until they are familiar with tables such as that on page 24.

The first chapter of the language course, with all its exercises, should not occupy more than one week, or we shall all become very weary of Marcel Duval and Señor Carrasco. Nevertheless, as much repetition as is possible without boredom should be aimed at. Our methods should conform to natural processes: a child, acquiring a new word, 'works' it until its use is almost automatic. Similarly, we shall 'work' each new word till the processes of mental translation are whittled away.

(iii) *Written Work*

Every first-year class, whether or no it will one day be subjected to written examinations, should write at least

one weekly exercise—the short grammatical item to reinforce its knowledge of the mechanics of the language; the
dictation, fulfilling the same purpose and securing relationship between sound and letter; the composition,
achieving all these and also the orderly arrangement of
ideas. A good composition, indeed, is a piece of creative
art, to be compared with the construction of a town, the
main street being extended and skilfully ramified in every
direction.

At this stage the composition is the culminating point
of the chapter; and deserves a further word or two. Let
the class, in class, write its composition from a skeleton
plan (*Charles, Marcelle enfants—demeurer Paris = Charles et
Marcelle sont des (deux) enfants qui demeurent à Paris*); at
home, having surrendered the text-book; or communally
(which should please those theorists who claim that an
excess of marks, rewards, and punishments at school is
the preparation for unbridled *laisser-faire* capitalism).
With a communal effort, each pupil makes his contribution, which is written on the board, and copied down by
the class. Interest is caused if an occasional mistake is
purposely made by the teacher, for correction by the
sharp-witted. The point of such correction must be
emphasized, or there is a risk that the error will take root
—but the rare pleasure of correcting, instead of being
corrected, probably compensates the pupil for this slight
danger.

(iv) *Correction of Written Work*

The class has now read its first chapter and produced
its first exercise and dictation. These can be marked by
the class itself from book or blackboard, leaving the essay
to the teacher. (If he works in a grammar school, he will
probably deal in piles of thirty—that mystic and traditional number so fixed, as a cynic has informed us, to give

him the greatest possible burden without encouraging his desire for revolt.) The evening school lecturer will be more fortunate; but some secondary modern schools, I believe, contain classes of forty, and these will become larger, at any rate for a time.

The principle of marking, I suggest, is not to *correct* the mistake, but to *indicate* it—to lead the writer back to first principles, to stimulate his thought processes. A correction of this sort, blindly copied by the pupil, is of slight value only:

> *mangeons*   *petits*   *dit Jean*
> "Nous mangons nos petit pains à 8 heures," Jean dit.

Correct as follows:

> V   A
> "Nous mangons nos petit pains à 8 heures," Jean dit.

What is gained?

Firstly, an unintelligent pupil might imagine that the first person plural ending of the present tense was always **-eons**; later we should have a rich crop of *nous joueons*, *nous commenceons*, *nous eteons* even; whereas he is now referred back to his memory, to the book, or to his own notebook, where almost certainly the **-ger** principle is laid down.

Secondly, we are reminding the writer about agreement (*A = Accord*). We cannot afford to do his work for him, still less let him infer that the adjective is invariably *petits* (by analogy with *gros*, *bas*, etc.).

Thirdly, a *numbered* footnote or marginal note (wide margins must be insisted on for this purpose) will remind the writer of inversion after the inverted commas (*cf.* "Go!" said he). The class should have a key to the various signs, devised to show the foreign equivalents of words such as 'Agreement,' 'Verb,' 'Mood,' etc.

I will agree that, by this method, correction by the pupil is not automatic; that the corrected work may still contain errors. Before marking the next exercise the teacher will have to survey the corrections of the last one and, if necessary, require some further amendments.

This will be obviated if a fairly generous time is given in class for corrections. The teacher should circulate, watching over the weak, moving to others when they cry "*Je ne comprends pas*"; "*Ich verstehe nicht*"; "*No entiendo*."

Prevention being simpler than cure, why not have each learner write his composition with a reminder-card before him? This card (or the same instructions could figure on the inside cover of his exercise book) would say, in English, for the benefit of the French learner:

HAVE I

made every adjective agree?
made my verb agree with its subject?
put my personal pronouns before all parts of the verb (except with affirmative commands), etc.?

The German sheet will say:

HAVE I

my verb at the end of the dependent clause?
after the adverb, put my verb before the subject, etc.?

(v) *Treatment of Grammar*

There are many ways of putting over grammar, and we all have our ideas as to which points cause the most confusion, and how such confusion may be cleared away. I will simply mention a few methods; there is no reason why all should not be used, say, in teaching Relative or Personal Pronouns:

(*a*) Direct Explanation, preferably before a passage is read.

c

(*b*) Induction. The class constructs the grammar, *e.g.*, the present tense of a verb, agreement of adjectives or past participles, pronouns showing owner of a part of the body (*Je me lave les mains*). Save with very intelligent groups, it is unlikely that the whole story will be forthcoming.

(*c*) Conversation (see page 21). This cannot, of course, be complete, but it can prepare the class for future problems, or reinforce those already studied.

(*d*) Dialogues (see page 36). This method can be adapted to almost any topic.

(*e*) Grammar in Action. This is most effective in later years (see page 76) when syntax also falls to be studied, and the class can read or listen with a fair degree of ease. The principle involves finding examples, in the reader or in fresh stories or even in songs or hymns (see page 45), of points already studied, and writing them in a special section of the note-book. Questions can be asked, *e.g.*, why *retournés*? Why *le plus beau jardin* **de** *la ville*? Why **einer** *der Männer*?

Testing grammar at this stage is much better done via 'reform' exercises—*i.e.*, eliciting *rendez-le-lui* by replacement of nouns, and not via translation.

Next, there is the question of treatment of special topics in French and German:

(*a*) FRENCH

A. The Verb

In a leisurely course (*i.e.*, five years for the General Certificate), it would be best to avoid the Perfect in the first year; that is to say, to select a book that does so. The Present, Future and Imperative are quite capable of ensuring that the verb gets its due share of attention. During the first year, therefore, we can describe events in future time, but cannot comment on the past. On the conversation blackboard (see page 21) we shall be limited to a present tense that illuminates the immediate past (*e.g., j'essuie le tableau noir* = 'I have just cleaned the blackboard'); just as a present tense can describe the immediate future (*je pars*; *je vais partir*).

Each of the three tenses should be carefully learned as soon as introduced, but it will be useful for subsequent purposes if, during the year, a plan is compiled showing the relationship of the 'fathers' or 'roots' (Infinitive and Present) to the 'sons' or 'stems' (Future and Imperative: the Latin Future, of course, being a mere appendage of the Latin Infinitive: *cantare habeo* = *chanterai*). An asterisk shows irregularity:

Regular Verbs

(1) INFINITIVE	(2) PRESENT	(1) FUTURE	(2) IMPERATIVE
		-ai, -as, -a -ons, -ez, -ont	
porter	port-e, -es, -e, -ons, -ez, -ent	porterai	port-e, -ons, -ez
finir	fin-is, -is, -it, -issons, -issez -issent	finirai	fin-is, -issons, -issez
vendre	vend-s, -s, -, -ons, -ez, -ent	vendrai	vend-s, -ons, -ez

Irregular Verbs

aller	vais, vas, va, all-ons, -ez, vont	*irai	va(s), allons, allez

While on the subject of the verb, let me state a good principle: break up the lesson as far as possible. Try to avoid forty-five minutes of writing, or reading, or talking (particularly your own talking)—and what more useful than an occasional verb competition between two sides of a class? Such breaks can be employed at any time during the first three or four years, when new work is still coming in. (A: *"Quel est l'impératif, deuxième personne du singulier, du verbe finir?"* B: *"C'est 'finis.' Et maintenant, quel est le futur d'aller, même personne?"*)

B. The Personal Pronoun

It may be well to point out, first, how dreary and parrot-like are replies, in English, that make no use of personal pronouns:

> "Does his father give George presents?"
> "Yes, his father does give George presents."

We are at once reminded of one of those ancient songs, endlessly repetitive: "Can she make an Irish stew, Billy boy, Billy boy? Can she make an Irish stew, me Billy boy?" "She can make an Irish stew," etc. . . .

In insisting on the use of *le, la, les,* their similarity to the definite article will be noticed.

The conciseness of *lui, leur* ('to him,' 'to them'), can be noted, observing that the English often merely say *him* for *to him*—a point of future danger when translating from English.

When working personal pronouns, a kind of three-cornered conversation can be practised—and, since language learning is a matter of habit, practised regularly:

André, touche Jean!

> André to Jean: *Je te touche.*
> André to teacher: *Je le touche.*
> Jean to teacher: *Il me touche.*

Danielle, donne la plume à Simone!

    Danielle: *Je te la donne.*
               Je la lui donne.
    Simone: *Elle me la donne.*

Then, of course, there are various ways of remembering the order of the double pronoun:

Person: **1—2—3ᴰ—3ᴵᴺᴰ—y—en** (provided everyone is clear concerning the nature of Direct and Indirect objects).

Football Team:

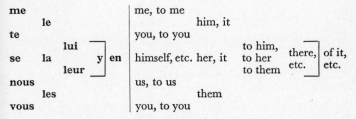

Perhaps a combination of the three methods is the only way to make sure of this extremely vital topic. Generally speaking, weaker classes need the dialogue method, with a rule or mnemonic as a quick reminder. They do not easily memorize word patterns; so the football team, of which most practising teachers are very tired, may be disbanded.

F–R–A–C—Friends, Relatives, Animals, Children—is a convenient mnemonic for the use of *tu* instead of *vous*. Custom, of course, varies in foreign families, but at least we can stipulate the use of *tu* when addressing younger relatives. Servants were once thought to merit *tu*, but the habit is perhaps dangerous at times of full employment. Pupils have great trouble in remembering to adhere to *tu* throughout a long passage—when writing a composition, for instance. Foreigners learning English, concerned only with 'you,' are much more fortunate. Some ascribe this to the fact that Britain has enjoyed, for some time, a greater measure of social equality than certain other European countries, and a relative freedom from snobbery.

(b) GERMAN

A. The Adjective

There is really no way of avoiding the morass of genders and plurals of nouns, and of cases of nouns and articles. Much steady practice is requisite. Indeed, coherent conversation in German is impossible until they are mastered. Further, the pupil becomes terribly discouraged by constant correction. So every device of encouragement, particularly with a moderate class, must be resorted to.

A useful visual aid, in the case of the adjective preceding the noun, is the following set of charts:

BETWEEN		BETWEEN		No ARTICLE
der *dieser* *jener* *welcher* } and noun		*ein* (sing. only) *kein* *mein,* etc. } and noun		

	M	F	N	Pl.		M	F	N	Pl.		M	F	N	Pl.
N		-e				-er	-e	-es						
A							-e	-es				as		
G			-en				-en					article		
D														

One should try to give some reason for such complexities or some analogy, rather than allow the pupil to feel himself a victim of pointless difficulties. It can be pointed out, for example, that German belongs to the same group of languages as Latin, and that it is still burdened with Latin case endings, though it soon merged the Ablative and Locative with the Genitive (*keineswegs* = 'in no way'). It can also be shown how Dutch (which is a half-way house between German and English) is similarly plagued—*der goede man*, for example. As boys at school, we would coin a sort of inflected adjective: *a fine-a fruit*, for example. The effect is similar, the cause different indeed.

B. Word-Order

What parallels can we find for the invariable rule that, in a main clause, the verb comes second? Take *das Dienstmädchen hält einen Löffel in der Hand*.

(*a*) Adverb-phrase first:

1	2	3	4
In der Hand	*hält*	*das Dienstmädchen*	*einen Löffel*

English gives us:

1	2	3
After the mayor	came	the aldermen

(*b*) Object first:

1	2	3	4
Einen Löffel	*hält*	*das Dienstmädchen in der Hand*	

—and in the well-known words of Yeats (*The Lake Isle of Innisfree*):

1	2	3	4	5
Nine bean rows	will	I	have	there

Poetry gives us many examples of adjectives, etc., at the start of a sentence, causing inversion (see, for instance, *The Winnowers*, by Robert Bridges).

The second precept, that the verb comes last in all dependent or relative clauses, has now no counterpart in English, but learners, unless they have studied Latin, find the separable verb at the end of the dependent clause a shade confusing: *er kann nicht verstehen, warum wir **weggehen*** seems an outrage, for one has heard that the separable prefix always comes at the end of the sentence.

When the dependent clause begins the sentence, we are back to our first rule, and the following pattern is useful:

Wenn, ... Vb/Vb . . . . . ., etc.

This, too, has no English parallel save, perhaps, in poetry, and then it is an incomplete one; but it deserves to be quoted:

> When, linnet-like confined, I
> With shriller throat shall sing. . . .
> (Lovelace, *To Althea from Prison*)

Finally, there is the rule that Past Participles and Infinitives come at the end of the sentence. This has given rise to innumerable quips about legendary Germans eeking to impose their own word-order on the English language ("Waiter, when do I a lamb chop become?"). To show the apparent vagaries of German, the class can, with advantage, translate a German passage into English, maintaining the original word-order. Probably, however, no one has better satirized the German language than Mark Twain, (*vide* his Appendix, *The Awful German Language*, to *A Tramp Abroad*).

I have heard it said that, German word-order being less automatic than our own, the writing of correct German needs that planned and orderly mind so characteristic of the Germans themselves. It is doubtful whether a large proportion of English children possess such a mind.

c. Prepositions

Before complaining too bitterly of the German preposition, let us remember that its English counterpart is equally exasperating. Except when it denotes a spatial relationship (the water 'under' the bridge), the use of a particular preposition is often impossible to justify. We sort things 'out,' count them 'up,' and look them 'over.' We say we are 'in' a temper, when the temper is 'in' us. (What of 'the bird is on the wing'?) We are 'under' a necessity, 'out' of patience, justified 'in,' delighted 'at,' worried 'by,' covered 'with.'

The chief points needing emphasis in German are:

(a) 'to' = *in, zu, nach, an, auf.* Use 'in' if 'into' is intended (*i.e.,* one finishes up 'inside' something).

Nach (lit., 'towards') for proper nouns (*er fährt nach Hamburg, fahren wir nach England!*) Break down the others with *zu* (for people: *komm zu mir*), *an* (for places: *er trat an die Tür*). *Auf* is rare (*auf die Universität, auf das Postamt,* etc.).

(b) *An* means, literally, 'along the surface of.' Hence *an der Wand, ich schreibe an die Wandtafel, Bonn liegt am Rhein, an der See*—in all such cases, one might tend to use *auf.*

(c) *Über,* with dative, is static. Conversely, we say *er fährt über die Berge.*

At the start of the course, it may be well to use wall charts, showing declensions of articles, adjectives, etc., and the cases after the principal prepositions (also, in French, the preceding adjectives, and the verbs taking *être*).

Lastly, no opportunity should be lost of showing 'grammar in action,' *e.g.,* among German songs, or tunes in the school hymnary, *Ein' feste Burg, Keine Schönheit hat die Welt, Der Tag bricht an, Nun lasst uns Gott dem Herren, Liebster Jesu,* and so forth. To this end, I have also used propaganda leaflets dropped on Nazi Germany, magazine advertisements, and even beer mats. In the search for realism, nothing should be despised.

(c) SPANISH

To reduce grammar to the minimum and to cash in on initial enthusiasm, one can:

(a) Omit *tu* and *vosotros* when conjugating verbs—though, like the German *du* and *ihr*, they will have to be brought in sooner or later. They may, of course, occur in early readers.

(b) Hold off the Past Definite tense until the Perfect has been thoroughly mastered.

Whatever the length of the course, however, no effort must be spared to control such items as *ser* and *estar* and the Personal Pronouns. Spanish and French are distinguished as much by their differences as by their similarities, and with these early points, oral examples may have to be reinforced by short translation questions.

Let us remember, however, that this grammar is but a means to an end, and that long tracts of grammar-with-sentences are the surest killers of interest. We are told that grammar was first systematized by Protagoras as recently as 450 B.C.; in other words, that men were able, for a very long time indeed, to learn languages without understanding their mechanism. It is a useful fact to bear in mind.

(vi) *Translation from English*

Why is translation into a foreign language the most painful and discouraging of all processes? It is surely that it relies on a series of grammatical abstractions. I myself am at sea with jargon such as "The world of matter, says Benedetto Croce, is abstracted by mind from the concrete experience of mind." This yields no visual picture. I can look at it for several minutes and retain none of it. So it is with the pupil called on to be aware of the fact that the past participle of a Reflexive Verb agrees with the Reflexive Pronoun—provided that this pronoun is a direct object.

Further, even when the rule has been assimilated, and it actually invokes such phrases as *elle s'est lavée, elle s'est lavé la figure* (a stumbling-block to many cultured Frenchmen), it is always liable to be driven from the mind by other abstractions, with the result that the pupil learns, but does not apply.

It is good psychology to let the pupil use, for as long as possible, *je travaille* (in answer to the question *travaillez-vous?*, or *que faites-vous?*) rather than cause him to produce *je suis travaillant* (when asked to translate *I am working*). And the same applies to *j'ai été parlant, écoutez-lui*, and similar horrors.

Whatever value translation possesses as a mental discipline is outweighed by the discouragement it involves for moderate pupils. Further, it does not usually enrich one's stock of words and expressions, but folds us back on ourselves. Then there is the search for suitable material for translation exercises, resulting in that strange jargon so insulting to our common sense: 'Who has the old owl?,' 'I died,' 'Was the admiral's face blue?,' 'Let us be born,' 'Do not let us be born.'

To sum up: as far as possible, keep translation from English out of the first year. The enthusiasm that usually marks a new study must be kept alive as long as possible.

6. POINTS OF PROCEDURE

(i) *Conservation of Energy*

Modern languages make very great demands on the teacher's energy: one is inclined to suggest that, like certain P.T. instructors, he should have a subsidiary qualification in some quiet subject, which he can teach between the years of forty-five and sixty-five. Afternoon periods should therefore be spent fairly restfully (*e.g.*, in reading, dictating, or testing). There is no point in leaving the explanation of difficult points to the after-dinner period, when the energy of one's pupils is hampered by digestive difficulties. Excessive enthusiasm is, after all, as wearing to one's classes as to oneself; a fact that Rostand ignored in *La Princesse lointaine*:

> Ah! l'inertie est le seul vice, Maître Erasme,
> Et la seule vertu, c'est . . . l'enthousiasme.

(ii) *Group Work*

We have already noted the value of communal effort: and another method, whereby the demon of competition may be exorcised, is that of working in pairs. Almost any exercise, but particularly anything resembling free composition, is suited to this method. Two similar brains are usually better than one; or, alternatively, the bright may assist the mediocre. The teacher can walk round, explaining his corrections to each pair; and it is, of course, a great advantage to be able to correct errors as they arise. I have even, in a little class, had small blackboards strung up around the walls, with pairs of pupils writing on them —the whole operation, of course, being controlled at the centre. (I cannot pretend, of course, that this makes for that solemn silence which is sometimes considered to be the hallmark of good teaching.) The method is rather more fully developed on page 51.

(iii) *Learning by Heart*

What is the effect of learning by heart on the linguist? Much depends on the retentiveness of the individual which is, in any case, comparatively low after the age of eleven. In the next few years, more and more facts will be jostling one another for inclusion in his memory.

In the main, a paragraph of a foreign language learned
by heart is retained only long enough for it to be, say,
incorporated in an essay a few days later. Nor does
learning by heart create a good memory, any more than,
say, the study of Greek teaches anything but skill in Greek.
I feel sure that many a modern Mrs Feather will have
learned, when at X County School for Girls, immense
portions of Longfellow and Keats, now forgotten. Sher-
lock Holmes was probably right when he told Watson
that the brain was an attic with limited space, and that
old junk must be turned out to accommodate new matter.
Abler pupils, of course, can store up many a quotation or
passage for future use; but even here, it is optimistic to
expect them to produce it at the right time.

(iv) *Gilding the Pill*

No teacher can afford to dispense with French, Spanish
and German songs, particularly the last-named, though
the class-room environment may make them seem a little
incongruous: twenty-four respectable schoolgirls singing
La Madelon or *Trink, trink, Brüderlein, trink*, would have
delighted the heart of W. J. Locke's Aristide Pujol, whose
educational adventures at a North London seminary for
young women must be read by all language teachers. . . .
Let the circumstances of the song, and its vocabulary be
introduced first: and break up a lengthy song (*e.g., Il
était un petit Navire*) by having different sections of the
class sing different verses. For a modest salary, we require
so much of the language teacher that it seems hard to
expect from him a good singing voice: if he does not
possess this, one of his class should be able to provide
the tune.

A gramophone has two main uses at this stage. One
is, of course, to offer recordings of simple songs, of which
a copy has already been shown to the class. The other

is, by way of variation of the teacher's voice, to present a native speaker whose accent can be imitated by the class, during suitable intervals on the disc. Pupils accustomed to a male teacher's voice ought sometimes to hear a woman, and *vice versa*. The opening chapters of many courses are now recorded.

Clearly, there are two essentials: a recorded speaker whose accent resembles the teacher's, and a faultless instrument. It is not common to find either.

If a recorded version of a simple story can be found, it can be played over, and the story written in exercise books from a plan on the blackboard.

Tape Recorders: When these become cheaper, they will no doubt be an essential item in every modern language room. They are particularly suitable for recording wireless programmes, conversations with foreign visitors, etc., but their value in improving pronunciation, by playing back pupils' voices, would seem to be limited to small groups.

Film strips are another device that both stimulates and educates. They can offer us excellent background pictures; and there are many other features that they could be made to provide—for instance, illustrated stories, and some of the sports, advertisements, famous characters, etc., of the country concerned. There is obviously great scope for development here of short features suitable for ending a lesson, but not for replacing it entirely.

Films, unless made specially for first-year work, are likely to have a highly discouraging effect. The only films that can conceivably be of value at this stage are:

(*a*) Silent 'background' films.
(*b*) Talkies, slowly pronounced, whose script has been seen and perhaps memorized in advance.

Zealous teachers who take their first-year people to a

foreign film, run by the local film society, may undo all their patient work in the classroom. The eleven-year-old who flattered himself he could understand reasonably well, is often lifted into another and incomprehensible world, with rapid or colloquial speech, or provincial accents.

Plays performed by visiting continental actors may have the same effect as adult films. Plays specially written for the classroom are well enough; and the characters can be dressed without appearing too incongruous against a background consisting of a blackboard and a shelf of geometry books. Come to that, almost any story forming part of a course or reader can be dramatized in part or in whole.

(v) *Vocabulary*

We ought, naturally, to base our courses on a system of word frequency, for example, the 500 or so most common words in the first year, the next 500 in the second year and so on. (The accuracy of any given system, like the cost of living index, may be open to question.) Readers, too, can be based on word frequency; and presumably they will be so graduated that there are not three or four new words on every line, exhausting the pupil, and killing his interest. While agreeing that, in almost any language, a cat is more important than a cassowary, a dish more serviceable than a distaff, I cannot see that we need be limited by official word counts. I favour yearly lists of useful words under special headings—radio, cars, bicycles, trains, furniture, etc. This can involve some drawing, and a link with the technical interests of the day.

A little etymology will also be well received, even at this early stage. (See also page 61.)

(vi) *Conclusion*

It only remains to stress fidelity to the principle of language-for-use, and not to relapse weakly into grammar and translations. The oral method may only add five per cent to general efficiency, but there is, after all, more to teaching than success in examinations. As Jespersen has remarked, the crammed examinee differs only from a crammed goose in that he fails to assimilate his diet.

It is true that some of the staunchest disciples of "language for use" have been foreigners, such as Jespersen himself, for many of whose pupils a fluent knowledge of English was an economic necessity. But even on a commonsense basis, it is clear that language is not a matter of forming a sentence from its component parts; that *wer ist an der Reihe?* and *je crois que non* will not emerge as a result of translation; that *Bier* and 'beer' are doubtful equivalents; and that conversation, in school before the Oral Examiner, or at some French *douane*, is either born of automatic reflexes, or still-born.

In offering these few suggestions for first-year teaching, I have disregarded all those topics that probably belong to general works, such as keeping a class in order, using a board to the best advantage, helping those who have been absent, keeping the sharper ones busy while assisting the backward, and so forth. Most of them relate to commonsense, personality, quick-wittedness, energy, determination, and the other intangibles required of a successful teacher. Without them, the niceties of method are completely vain.

Chapter Three

THE MIDDLE SCHOOL

THIS, for our purpose, represents the middle three years of a five-year course, or the second and third year of a four-year course. We must admit that it is often the graveyard of many hopes and aspirations. What was begun at the age of eleven or thereabouts may already seem stale; oral methods have given way to 'grammar grind'; a dreary teacher has, perhaps, appeared on the scene; certain pupils have developed an inferiority complex, and are patiently waiting for the end.

Is this the time, then, to abandon utility and realism, teaching modern languages as some do the classics, and replacing interest by coercion? By no means; though some modification of our methods may be essential.

Much depends, of course, whether middle school classes are organized in sets. This would probably be commoner if more modern language teachers became principals.

If it is a matter of classes and not sets, then we may have to make increasing use of English; but, with sets, perhaps the lowest only need deviate from our theories. Why, in any case, should the poorer elements abandon the practice of French *via* French or Spanish *via* Spanish? The answers are many: the learners may be incapable of a sustained effort of understanding; they cannot follow any grammatical abstraction in another language; they cannot readily speak, there are too many mental processes between seeing or hearing and speaking, too many slips, as it were, between the eye, and the lip; they

D

may be unable to write the foreign language correctly, though they may excel in short grammar or vocabulary questions calling for brief and simple answers.

We shall, therefore, at the end of this chapter, deal specially with the problems of the 'C' or 'D' stream, if 'stream,' which suggests perpetual progress, is not too flattering a term.

Everything we have said in Chapter Two applies to the average middle school form. But here are some further developments:

1. COMPOSITION

As translation into English, in the form of written exercises, should not be attempted yet—it is often a prostitution of the mother tongue—our main efforts will be concerned with compositions (or essays) and, to a lesser extent, with translation from English. In the first year, the composition was tied very largely to the subject-matter in the course; this will still be the case, but the 'free' sector will be greatly extended. I shall mention various methods and functions of the composition:

(a) As an exercise in grammar. Take, for example, the introduction of the Subjunctive in French, which some courses offer us in the penultimate year—rather prematurely, as I sometimes think. It is not enough, when the subject is so *recherché*, so little practised via reading and conversation, to give notes; the Subjunctive, or what you will, should be consciously woven into the fabric of compositions. For the first two or three compositions, after the matter has been introduced, I invite my pupils to use a number of Subjunctives. They make claims, via asterisks in the margin, for each Subjunctive used. Such claims, if over-optimistic, will be disallowed, *e.g.*, if the insertion is inaccurate, or inappropriate. I seem to remember something like this:

* . . . il mourut en 1869, quoique sa mère fût Italienne

—a *non sequitur* that did not deserve to succeed.

(*b*) As oral practice. When a story has been read, the members of a class can be asked in turn to retell it. As each *raconteur* says his piece, a few words can be written on the board, serving as a plan for composition. With less progressive classes, the plan may precede and assist the spoken summary. The teacher can augment his pupil's remarks with sentences of his own. They note these down under some such heading as *Suggestions du Professeur,* or *Die Bemerkungen des Lehrers,* and learn them.

(*c*) As an exercise in co-operation. We have recommended (page 44) that a class should work in pairs—the habitual pairing being sometimes altered so as to place the dull with the bright. It is a device particularly suited to the middle school composition. Each pair, instead of each individual, then produces the essay. On the sheet allotted to each pair, I often have two margins drawn, one for corrections, one headed + and —, under which marks for good phrases and for errors are recorded. I correct as I go round (though I realize that there is not much space in many a classroom), and award points.

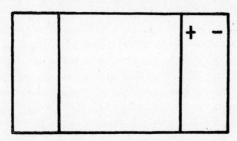

Duller children often learn much in the company of their betters, particularly if they write alternate sentences and are not sitting passively about, cashing in on their partners' brilliance. Some noise is inevitable when co-operation is substituted for competition, but perhaps excusable.

In every case, a parrot-like reproduction of the original story is not, of course, desirable; such a result is avoided, as we have seen, by the use of grammatical material, and also by the inclusion of fresh material of the writer's own choice. Such exercises give very general satisfaction to pupils—they are less confining than translations. However, it is an unfortunate fact that many examining bodies give less consideration to essays, free or reproductive, than to translation; difficulties of standardization are no doubt the principal cause.

2. GRAMMAR

Grammatical points are so adequately set out in books, and methods of putting them over are so diverse (see page 33), that there is point only in stressing two or three developments relevant to this stage:

(i) *The Conjugation of Verbs*

Children often return from school with substantial portions of learning work; but invariably, unless told how to do it, they have spent more time than was necessary. With verbs, the linchpin of the sentence in most foreign languages, it is well worth the trouble of simplifying the learner's task. In French particularly, all classes will benefit by *writing out* the verbs in orderly fashion, so as to show the relationship between root and stem.

Which tenses are requisite to which year is not for me to decide. In a five-year course, we shall normally need, in the Second Year, Present, Perfect, Future, Imperative; in the Third Year, the Present Participle will be introduced, along with the Imperfect, Pluperfect, and Conditional; in the Fourth Year, the Subjunctive is sometimes touched on. If, therefore, I append the full scheme as for the Fourth Year, (pp. 54–55) it will be understood that a more limited version is applicable to earlier years. The numbers show relationship of root and stem, a dagger indicates conjugation with *être*, an asterisk indicates irregularity: the order is that of Regular, Auxiliary, Irregular Verbs:

German irregular verbs rarely occasion the same trouble; partly, no doubt, because those who study a second language have already shown some skill with French: partly because so many of our own weak and strong verbs follow the German pattern. There is real difficulty, however, in the modification of certain strong verbs in the 2nd and 3rd person (singular) of the Present Tense. As a youth in Wembley, I used to admire the skill of a speedway rider named L A M O R E AU X. I little realized how useful the vowels of his name might be. In German, strong verbs usually indicate a vowel change, though not necessarily in the Imperative:

A	*ä*	*a* (in Imperative)
O	*ö*	*o* (in Imperative)
E	*ie* (*e.g.*, *sehen*) *i* (*e.g.*, *nehmen*)	
AU	*äu*	*au* (in Imperative)

Let the weak verbs whose Infinitive ends in *-den*, *-ten*, be specially noted, with their *-est*, *-et* (Present Tense), their *-ete*, etc. (Imperfect).

(ii) *The Use of Past Tenses*

Since German has one past tense fewer than French, its Imperfect having a double function, it is with the French trio, Perfect, Past Historic, and Imperfect, that we have to deal. In the third year, the pupil who knows all about *il*

1 INFINITIF	2 PART. PRÉSENT	3 PART. PASSÉ	4 PRÉSENT	5 P. HISTORIQUE
				-ai -as -a -âmes -âtes -èrent / -is -is -it -îmes -îtes -irent / -us -us -ut -ûmes -ûtes -urent
porter	portant	porté	port-e -es -e -ons -ez -ent	portai (portas)
finir	finissant	fini	fin-is -is -it -issons -issez -issent	finis
vendre	vendant	vendu	vend-s -s - -ons -ez -ent	vendis
avoir	ayant	eu	ai as a av-ons -ez ont	eus
être	étant	été	suis es est sommes êtes sont	fus
†aller	allant	allé	v-ais -as -a all-ons -ez vont	allai

1 FUTUR	1 CONDITIONNEL	2 IMPARFAIT	2 SUBJ. PRÉS.	3 PARFAIT	4 IMPÉRATIF	5 SUBJ. IMPARF.
-ai	-ais	-ais	-e			-se
-as	-ais	-ais	-es			-ses
-a	-ait	-ait	-e			-̂t
-ons	-ions	-ions	-ions			-sions
-ez	-iez	-iez	-iez			-siez
-ont	-aient	-aient	-ent			-sent
porterai	porterais	portais	porte	j'ai porté	porte! portons! portez	portasse
finirai	finirais	finissais	finisse	j'ai fini	finis! finissons! finissez!	finisse
vendrai	vendrais	vendais	vende	j'ai vendu	vends! vendons! vendez!	vendisse
*aurai	*aurais	avais	*ai-e -es -t ay-ons -ez aient	j'ai eu	*aie! ayons! ayez!	eusse
*serai	*serais	étais	*sois-s -s -t soy-ons -ez soient	j'ai été	*sois! soyons! soyez!	fusse
*irai	*irais	allais	*aill-e -es -e all-ions -iez aillent	je suis allé	va(s)! allons! allez!	allasse

a chanté—il chanta—il chantait may still have his essays and translations spattered with the tell-tale sign T (wrong tense).

What is the key to the problem? The old primers informed us that the three tenses meant 'he has sung' (or 'he sang'); 'he sang'; 'he was singing' ('used to sing,' 'would sing'). That did not see us through in such sentences for translation as 'It was morning; the larks sang in the heavens,' or ' "She left yesterday," he said.' Nor was the matter resolved in essays, where even more problems arise.

As a matter of fact, the tense difficulty is comparatively slight in translation. One can use a mnemonic "Let Norman Come Down" which, being interpreted, means that the Perfect is generally used for the events in Letters, Newspapers, Conversation, Diaries—apart from which, the Past Historic is requisite in narrative. (Incidentally, the Past Historic is surely a better title than Past Definite, for it suggests a contrast with the recent events of the Perfect, which might also be styled Recent Past.) The Perfect, on account of its difficulties, should be avoided unless there is evidence that the passage has some connection with letters, newspapers, conversation and diaries. An essay written in the First Person, however, may be assumed to derive from one of these. Nobody wants such stuff as *nous vînmes à un café et mangeâmes notre goûter*. The Imperfect, for its part, can be used for actions, or states of mind, which were habitual or not completed at that time.

These things, however, are not easy to determine. What of the following passage?

> Arabella's birthday came. She sat by the window reading her letters. When George saw her, he felt pleased, for she looked so pretty. For a long time he tried to explain what his sister wanted but it was in vain.

What is a typical member of 4B to make of this? 'Sat,' 'felt,' 'tried,' 'wanted'—were these habitual, or unfinished at that particular moment?

It is wise, I think, to make these conditions subsidiary, and rather to ask ourselves, of a given verb in the past tense, whether it represents the Next Event in the story or narrative, or whether it had been going on previously. By such a test, 'came'—'saw'—'felt'—'tried'—'was' are the 'next' events. (It wants a little acumen to realize that 'sat' is not an event at all, had been going on for some time when George arrived.) 'Looked' is a little dubious—but presumably she was pretty BEFORE George came in, that is to say, to all comers? 'Tried' is a poser, until it is understood that the duration of the action is not a factor at all, *i.e.*, all the following would count as 'next' events: 'he left England, he arrived in Paris, he spent forty-four years there, he returned to London.' 'Was in vain' may trouble some of us, until people grasp that the next Emotion, the next State of Affairs, the next State of Mind, are all considered to be events. (Studying languages in classrooms is too often a matter of nailing together two supposed equivalents, such as 'was' and *était*. People forget circumstances such as *en me voyant, il fut surpris*.)

Similarly, by lightly labelling the Imperfect as the Descriptive Tense, they perpetuate phrases such as *puis il commençait à neiger*.

The middle school essay, as we have said, will more often be a reproduction of something read (by teacher or class), than a completely free composition. A board plan not only gives sequence and shape, but can be immensely helpful at the time when past tenses are being learned. Here, for example, is that well-known story about two hunchback tailors Pierre and Paul, the former an upright character, the latter undesirable. Pierre closed the shop one evening, made his way home. It was a fine evening. He passed a field where some dwarfs were singing *lundi, mardi, mercredi* (a theme not notably more inane than many of the present day). He watched them, and mentioned that their song was not complete; that they should add *jeudi et puis vendredi*. Pleased with this, since it rhymed, they removed his hump with a magic ointment. The next night, Paul, who wishes for a similar reward, adds a third line, *samedi et puis dimanche*. This fails to rhyme, and he gets a second hump for his pains. Here are two possible plans that follow the pattern of the story, and show which past tenses are appropriate:

Imparfait	*Parfait*
Deux bossus, Pierre et Paul	
Pierre (être) gentil, Paul méchant	
(être) tailleurs	
	Un soir Pierre (fermer) boutique
	(Retourner) chez lui
(Faire) beau temps lune (briller)	
	(Passer) par champ
Nains (danser) (chanter)	
	Pierre (regarder), (dire) "chanson pas finie"
	(Ajouter), *etc.*

In diagram form, we can offer the following picture (the main line represents the Perfect, the branch lines the Imperfect. To go down the latter halts progress, of course. We must, this time, *begin* with a Perfect):

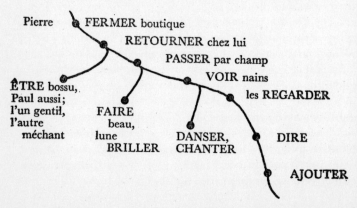

If time allows, the story can be read off first, with additions to suit the taste of the speaker. There will, of course, be the pupil who translates in his mind, and renders 'he saw' by *il vu*. He needs to be told that the French Perfect has an extra word; we cannot expect him to couple it with the English 'he has seen.'

The same plans can, of course, be used when the Past Historic has been mastered.

3. TRANSLATION FROM ENGLISH

The middle years of the language course will almost certainly call for some translation into French, German, or Spanish. Even an able class or set of small dimensions will find translation exercises in its course; pupils having, by now, a fair command of the language, translation will not be unduly laborious, and it is impossible to disregard the fact that public examinations are largely based on translation, a fact often regretted by teachers of the Direct method. These translations may be written in class or at home, and corrected; or done orally, spelling being insisted on where doubt may arise (*e.g.*, with French verb endings, etc.) I sometimes stage a French lesson entitled *Cherchez les fautes*. The less able are 'put on.' I copy their efforts on the board, occasionally making intentional errors. Or we have a class effort on the board, with a spare column on the right-hand side, wherein useful words and expressions suggested by the text can be written.

Useful translation material, over and above that suggested by the course, may be based on the pupil's mistakes in essays, etc. In French one should keep a list of these, entitled *Difficultés*; and short sentences of not more than eight words in length, containing such points, can be bandied to and fro between competing sides. Such 'snags' will vary from class to class, and there is little point in citing sixty or seventy of them.

4. CONVERSATION

Apart from the daily class business being conducted, where possible, in the foreign language (see pages 20–22—such phrases should constantly be added to), some questions and answers under certain headings, and some specialized vocabulary should now be attempted. It may be found useful to have a notebook for this purpose—the *Carnet moderne* or *Carnet de Conversation*, for example, or the *Unterhaltungsheft*. Question and answer should be set out on left and right hand pages:

Combien de pièces avez-vous à la maison ?	**Nous en avons huit, c'est-à-dire, un salon, une cuisine, une salle à manger, trois chambres à coucher, une salle de bain, des cabinets**
Sind Sie je ins Ausland gegangen?	*Ja, ich bin nach Frankreich gegangen: nie bin ich in Deutschland, oder in Spanien, oder in Italien gewesen,* etc.

Who would speak a language must first murder it, and it may as well be murdered to some purpose, that is to say, in connection with useful topics, such as are not always found in school text-books.

More conversation arises out of *Lecture expliquée*, where two or three questions, after a given piece of reading, can be asked by anyone in the class: or someone, conveniently called *Le Professeur*, or *Der Lehrer*, may occupy a desk on the dais, putting his queries and giving the usual questioner a rest.

An occasional piece of reading may be dramatized: a portion of narrative such as:

"Elle lui demanda de lui acheter un parapluie; mais il refusa, avec mille regrets"

—turned into direct speech between two participants.

A good class or set will also be able to make something
out of a given 'situation.' "You are lost in Berlin—ask
Patricia the way to the Anhalter Station. Patricia will
direct you," etc.

5. Miscellaneous Points

(i) *Etymology*

Explanations of grammar, or the learning of new words,
are always helped and brightened by the use of etymology.
At an early stage, the connection between the French
circumflex accent and an -*s* omitted (*forêt*, 'forest') will
have been noted; so, too, will the possible substitution
of -*s* for the prosthetic -*e* (*école*, 'school'). Children studying both Latin and French can watch the Roman invasion
at work (**bovem**—*bœuf*; **aquam**—*eau*—eyebrows will be
raised at this, the Latin word having undergone a drastic
change that is still keeping scholars busy): the Teutonic
invasion is less well known (**vadum**—*gué*). There's a bit
of sociology in 'mutton' growing up side by side with the
more pedestrian 'sheep,' 'pork' with 'pig.' Those learning
German like to hear about the Dutch language, an
interesting link between German and English (**Kaffee**—
Koffie—'coffee'); and such similarities as *wäre er hier* and
'were he here' (a case of using the Subjunctive, Jourdain-
like, without knowing it).

'He went under,' 'he underwent,' will show German
separable and inseparable verbs in action. One should
mention the relationship between Latin and German
verb endings and Genitives, and say why German verbs in
dependent clauses normally go to the end of the sentence.
To show the same simple sentence in High and Low
German, Swiss German, Yiddish, and Pennsylvania
Dutch, is also of some interest. So, too, are local Anglo-
Saxon, or nineteenth-century German emigré survivals,

such as 'twitten' or 'twitchell' (*zwischen*), a narrow passage.

Words from any language (*débris, Kindergarten, tornado*), embodied in our own, are always worth collecting.

(ii) *Learning by Heart*

Learning by heart of connected passages or sets of phrases has, as we have seen (p. 44), a somewhat limited value. It is an unpopular task; it has yet to be proved that it makes for an orderly mind; and it should, ideally, be tested both in speech and in writing—those learning a passage containing a phrase such as *elle devait se lever*, repeating it to themselves later, may well be saying, in effect, *elle devait se levé* and enshrining a wrong principle. At this level, then, for the benefit of those with indifferent memories, one should tend to set portions of a foreign language, the learning of which will subsequently be reinforced by oral and written use.

(iii) *The Second Modern Language*

During the middle years, a second modern language may perhaps be chosen. We have already considered the suitability of certain competing languages (see page 15). Much depends, however, on the other languages already studied. Perhaps Latin and French are already in progress, in which case a third language is only to be considered for very able people with high Intelligence Quotient: whether this third language be classical or modern depends on a whole range of factors, one of which is the candidate's disposition, *e.g.*, whether he is lively and fond of oral work. Of two modern languages, French and German represent two varied techniques; French and Spanish together would probably offer fewer problems, especially if the second is begun much later than the first. (I took up Italian and Spanish at about the same time, and once had a very uncomfortable evening at a social, with an Italian on one side of me, and a Spaniard on the other.) As an examiner, I have often found signs of the same discomfort, notably in the work of candidates who have started French, Latin, and Spanish within a short time of each other and who, therefore, confuse them deplorably.

French and German, of course, contain many more similarities than is generally supposed (e.g., *du hast Recht, sagte er; was will er tun?; sie hat ihm den Zylinder vom Kopfe gestossen*, etc.), and these should always be commented on as they arise.

There is no reason why German should not be begun before French—save that Ordinary Level papers usually require five years' work in the latter, as opposed to three or four in the former.

When the second language is a year old, it is often enjoyable to translate from it, not into English, but into the first foreign language.

A second language is often best left until two or three years before taking the Advanced examination; the consequent saving of time by able performers is surely an important factor. By then, the sixth-former knows why he is working, and what he is working for—this cannot always be said of younger pupils. Intensive courses in the sixth form may be compared with new subjects begun at the university—though one may be at a disadvantage when competing with others who have begun earlier. I have, however, managed to prepare sixth-form candidates for 'Ordinary' Level Spanish in six months: and the thought of the time wasted by clever people in three-year courses is disquieting.

(iv) *Songs*

A small point should be added to my remarks on page 45. The vocabulary of the songs ought not to be too unusual, nor the tenses outside the compass of experience. For example, French songs should not contain the Past Historic until that tense arises. Some songs will support a tense change, *e.g.*, *elle fit un fromage*, from *Il était une Bergère*, may be altered to *elle a fait un fromage*. Some think that French songs tend to lack virility for the middle school pupil, and offset this by putting French words to English tunes, or even by translating famous English songs into French. It would indeed be curious to hear *On Ilkla' Moor* sung in the language of Flaubert.

(v) Games

When monotony threatens, the following may be resorted to:

(a) *Team Translation:* Two boards, on which two people, one from each team, translate the same sentence.

(b) *German Football League:* Each member of the group plays each other member. An English-German sentence, illustrating current difficulties and containing not more than 8–10 words, is given, and the setter's goals are the mistakes of his adversary. An up-to-date League Table is kept, whereon the leader of a group of eight might finish as follows:

	Played	Won	Drawn	Lost	Goals For	Against	Points
Anstruther:	7	5	1	1	19	6	11

(The game is, of course, applicable to any language where the numbers studying it are small.)

(c) Making as many words as possible with longer words such as *considérable*, *Streichholzschachtelchen* (longer words counting double). Those giving out their words can be asked to spell them in

French or German. Alternatively, verbs only can be asked for, in which case the Tense and Infinitive should also be supplied.

(d) Any variation of the *Twenty Questions* theme.

(e) *Completing Pictures*—*e.g.*, of trains, cars, faces, dress, etc. One can draw a carriage on the board; and successive people can come forward and add an item, writing its name on the board, till a complete train is constructed. Items can also be named as they are rubbed off.

6. WEAKER FORMS

(i) *A Special Problem*

Form 3D, or whatever it may be called, is not only a linguistic, but a national problem. Its thirty-odd apathetic or turbulent people often form a kind of grammar-school proletariat, and there is no accepted way of dealing with them. Some, claiming that about twenty-five per cent of the grammar-school population are wasting their time, would educate them in other secondary schools, or at least transfer them if they become bored and ineffective, or acquiesce in their leaving at fifteen; others feel that they can do respectably if driven sufficiently hard; still others would keep them where they are, modifying time-table and teaching methods to suit them.

If these people are organized in large forms, and not sets, they may well reveal a marked range of ability: they have almost certainly lost interest (especially if they began the subject before the age of 11+, or are taking six years instead of five to progress to Ordinary Level); they possibly have a feeling that they will never undergo a public examination; worse, they are often in the hands of the least skilful teachers—whereas, heaven knows! they need the best. Sometimes, as we have seen, they are found to be studying two foreign languages, to the considerable confusion of both.

To these psychological and administrative disadvantages must be added the mental limitations of the children themselves. Most probably:

(*a*) They will be poor at grasping any kind of abstraction (*e.g.*, what a Past Participle is, and, what is worse, how it behaves).

(*b*) They will have poor memories (save for incidents or activities they particularly desire to remember).

(*c*) They will be unable to concentrate for long, at least on one matter or topic.

(*d*) They will find it hard to co-ordinate brain and muscle: thus they will pronounce well in imitation, less well in reading.

(*e*) They have a sharp sense of their own inferiority —whether they be called 3D or 3A (after Miss Attleborough, their form teacher).

(*f*) Unable to do much with a foreign language, they may feel it to be, for them, a useless study.

The following are, I think, the principles that have to be borne in mind, in order to counter these failings. There is, as yet, no certainty that any members of 3D will abandon the language at the end of the year; nor is any new test at the Ordinary Level examination yet in sight:

(ii) *The Solution of the Problem*

(*a*) Grammatical rules must not be handed out as such; examples of them, on the other hand, must be constantly spoken and written, wherein the principle can be shown at work. Yet there must be a minimum of such grammar.

(*b*) There must be a vast amount of repetition, a cautious increase of vocabulary and grammar; much testing, but in a variety of guises.

(*c*) Periods will be artfully broken up to allow of different activities.

(*d*) There may be some sacrifice of oral accuracy to fluency.

(*e*) Encouragement, rather than captious criticism, will be the teacher's policy.

(*f*) The practical value of the foreign language will be incessantly shown.

(iii) *Detailed Treatment*

(*a*) Grammar

A statement to the effect that "French possessive pronouns agree with the object, and not the owner" is colourless and tiresome. Far better to post the list of pronouns, then to announce, with appropriate gestures, *mes souliers sont noirs, les vôtres sont bruns* (*vide* the Dialogue Method in the First Year, page 36). Further examples should then be asked for. After each, insert the principle. Each day, subsequently, comes the question. *Quelle est la différence entre votre nez et le sien?*—the principle being mentioned *after* the reply. In due course the principle will be established, if and when translation into French is embarked upon. (Incidentally, French pronouns, *cela, le mien, ce que, lequel*, and the rest of them give rise to such confusion that there cannot be too many dialogues about them.)

(*b*) Repetition

Repetition, disguised in a variety of forms, is the sole guarantee of success; and courses which wantonly introduce fresh grammar, not to mention readers full of rare words, make the process difficult.

Testing, though necessary, must not take up so much of the period that the pupil has no time for correction, or becomes bored. Nor should the manner of testing always remain the same. Testing vocabulary or verbs may take the following forms—orally, round a class; on slips of paper; pupils move up and down the line, according to success or failure; questions by the class itself, divided into two or more sides. In the last resort, testing arises from disbelief in the capacity or industry of a given set of individuals; and if there is reason to think that this is a pessimistic view, the testing can be waived.

(c) Variety

Ideally, no activity should absorb the whole period: there are, after all, the following pursuits on which changes can be rung—reading, conversation, writing, exposition, acting (of plays or dramatized prose passages), Grammar in Action (see page 76), singing, scrap-books or similar activities (see pages 26, 88), illustrated word-lists (planes, cars, etc.), private reading, games. And even these divisions can be broken down—for instance, conversation can consist of question and answer, impromptu speeches; written work may be an individual prose or essay, competition between two groups, or work written by one pupil in public while others do the same on their papers. Then it is a question of "Cherchez la faute!" (see page 59). An able teacher will use all these activities in orderly progression, and some of these will ensure that, for a few blessed minutes, he himself stops talking.

(d) Accuracy versus Fluency

By this time, the typical member of 3D may have lost the feeling that it is fun to talk—the words come so laboriously to mind, or not at all; when they do, he is reluctant to utter them. The teacher must therefore coax, persuade, stimulate. What acts as a stimulus? A realistic course; good question and answer material (see page 60), worked so often that its use becomes automatic; phrases for classroom use (see pages 21–23); glossing over certain mistakes in the interests of fluency; and credit, given on the spot, or assessed periodically, for good work.

This done, and a good 'oral atmosphere' provided, the teacher can now exact his price—periods, or parts of periods, when only the foreign language may be spoken; and penalties, for those who use English.

(e) Encouragement

Anyone venturing to teach 3D must be robust, active, humorous, firm yet friendly, encouraging rather than captious: by no means everybody combines these qualities. In particular he or she must know how his pupils' minds work. Encouragement will take various forms: generosity (but not of a foolish kind) with marks and with praise; passing over errors (see *Accuracy versus Fluency*, Section (d) above) if the culprit knows no better, and has at least used the brain (*e.g., vous iriez blanc; je le veux venir*); taking a few minutes after hours to go over a disastrous script with the writer; assigning a dull absentee to the best pupil in the form, who can aid him after hours—for example, with a 'prose' correction he has missed; occasional sub-division of the group, so as to hearten and instruct the very poor; and some lightening of the load by:

A. Limiting the 'active' type of test, *e.g.*, prose translation, and concentrating on 'passive' and reproductive work.

B. Arranging that harder tests, such as translation from English and dictations are pre-prepared, *e.g.*, a translation is "run over" in class before a homework, and a dictation is read at home before being worked in class. Similarly, passages learned by heart can be utilized in compositions, where, in any case, only the simplest language should be used.

c. Waiving rare rules and exceptions. (Sweet, in his *Practical Study of Languages*, records having to learn the word *Hornung* (February), as constituting the one exception to the rule that nouns ending in *-ung* are feminine. For years he treasured this bit of knowledge, but when at last he met the word, he had forgotten all about its peculiarities.) Better to get the plural of *hibou* wrong, than that the matter should crowd out something more useful.

(*f*) Practical Value

3D is strongly responsive to the idea that French or German is of practical value to them or to other people. To such a class, part of the grammar school routine is pure tedium; all the rewards and sanctions in the world will not produce sustained interest; there is an unspoken feeling that 'they,' for reasons unknown, have saddled 'us' with a course which may be good for our souls, but which has little or no connection with everyday life.

Let us stress the fact—via foreign visits and correspondence, successes (if any) of former 3D boys or girls with export firms, the presence of French, Belgian, German or Swiss Scouts or Guides at the local jamboree—that this language is useful to them, and may at any time become more so; by wall pictures, scrap books, visiting speakers, occasional readings of extracts dealing with foreigners and their lives, and gramophone records, we must show that here are real people living a few score miles away whom to meet is a commonplace, to understand is a necessity.

Chapter Four

THE FIRST EXAMINATION

1. THE NATURE OF THE TASK

(i) *Drawbacks of Present 'Ordinary' Papers*

THE first examination is, no doubt, a spur for the lazy, and an indication of progress: but, in its present form, it has many unsatisfactory features.

Most teachers agree on some or all of these features, but they do not do enough to make their opinions known. Examining Boards are by no means unreceptive to suggestions.

Firstly, the brevity of the oral examination, on grounds of expense, stultifies the 'direct' method of teaching. You do not have to pass in the oral language to secure a pass in a modern language, though some authorities do add oral to written marks, making them, perhaps, ten per cent of the whole. At Christmas, where there are fewer candidates, there is sometimes no oral examination at all. The teaching in the General Certificate year may often be undistinguishable from that of a dead language.

Secondly, the large amount of translation from the foreign language, sometimes counting about fifty per cent of the marks, involves a great deal of really bad English, as well as reducing the time in which the foreign language can be employed.

Thirdly, the examination is usually too hard for weaker candidates, and only a boring repetition of words and rules, having nothing whatever to do with the living language, offers any chance of success.

Fourthly, since it is for many the last year, it introduces an element of finality which is unfortunate, if languages at school are to have lasting value.

Fifthly, the issue of success or failure, which every examination presents, overshadows the course and stresses results at any cost.

I shall, later in the chapter, discuss alternative forms of the First Examination, suitable for weaker candidates. Meanwhile, we should see whether any modifications are desirable in the interests of the rank and file, and how the various sections of a typical paper may best be dealt with.

(ii) *Their Content*

Most examining boards require translation into English, sometimes of both prose and poetry; translation from English, usually of a prose passage; a free composition, based on a plan or sometimes on a story read in advance; a dictation; and an oral test, which usually constitutes a separate paper.

Let it be said straight away that we should have teaching that is at once more practical and more realistic if the oral examination counted fifteen per cent or even twenty per cent of the total marks.

It is also desirable to bring back the distinction mark, to furnish a stimulus for abler people. What effort would be forthcoming from university students, if they were merely called on to pass or fail? A distinction, furthermore, supplies a useful guide as to the subjects, if any, to be studied in the sixth form.

2. TEACHING SUGGESTIONS AND POSSIBLE MODIFICATIONS

(i) *Translation into English*

The boredom often associated with the 'Certificate' year —and it is particularly marked where there are no sets, or where pupils return, full of enthusiasm, from a foreign exchange, only to run into a course which has nothing in common with their experiences—could be mitigated by more intelligent work in this sphere. Open Ramsden and Holroyd's *School Certificate French* and you will find a series of unconnected extracts for translation into English, where authors, themes and centuries are jumbled together in hopeless confusion. One reads, with Daudet, of the approaching end of the little Dauphin: sympathy is aroused, but before the outcome is known, another piece must be begun. It is by Lichtenberger, and relates Trott's encounter with a snail.

If the study of individual extracts is necessary—and obviously, a continuous story is more likely to maintain interest—let them be arranged chronologically, with short notes on the author and the passage, and we have something to carry forward to the sixth-form course: or better, there might be a number of extracts from one book. (In any case, really capable pupils following a five-year course may be finding the fifth year somewhat tedious, and could well be doing plenty of private reading in class or at home, and getting a glimpse of next year's literature).

The English—if that is the word—produced by this translation process, has an oddly deadening effect. To listen to an oral translator saying, "after having meditated during some long hours, she promised to him that which he was asking" is to have one's critical sense stifled. Examiners should penalize this sort of thing, and it should not be possible to earn marks merely by stringing together single words, however correct individually.

In this connection, there does not seem much point in having poems translated into English prose, as commonly happens in German. Since poets play tricks with word-order, and create unusual images, a prose translation, whose writer is resolved to lose no marks for inaccuracy, is normally disastrous.

On the score of precision, I usually suggest the following points to ensure an *accurate* translation (failure in which is underlined singly):

(*a*) Read the entire passage before writing—the last line may throw light on the first.

(*b*) Leave no gaps: use your deductive powers, or try to find a similarity between the unknown word and one in English, French, or Latin.

(*c*) Translate a difficult sentence word for word on a piece of rough paper, and reassemble the words.

And here are some useful points of style to assist in banishing that lifeless stuff passing for English in many published translations, let alone in classroom scripts. Failure to observe them gets a double underline:

(*a*) Don't be bound by the foreign order of words and clauses.

(*b*) Punctuation: long sentences may be divided.

(*c*) Do not translate proper names (e.g., *Rue de la Madeleine*, rather than the incongruous mixture, *Madeleine Street*).

(*d*) Avoid direct equivalents (e.g., *demander* = 'demand,' *commencer* = 'commence'), as, of course, different associations grow up around cognate words. The equivalent is, therefore, often wrong or unsuitable. Generally speaking, the French equivalent of the Latin is less pedantic than ours (*descendere—descendre*—descend). The search for synonyms is, furthermore, good for one's English.

(*e*) Give the Imperfect tense its special value—the first time it appears, in the passage, at any rate.

There is no harm, of course, in learning by heart lists

of words for use in Unseens—many words, notably names of trees, flowers, articles of clothing, are almost impossible to deduce from the context, and the vocabulary at the back of a reader or course-book, suitably amended, is sometimes useful for the purpose. A note should be given about these words which could be wrongly used when translating back into the foreign language (e.g., *le duvet* = 'down'; *déménager* = 'to move,' etc.).

When the French–English or German–English word list has been learned, it can be revised in a number of ways. One can prepare a simple definition, in the foreign tongue, of 26 words, representing every initial letter from A to Z, putting these to the class, and rewarding the first person to call out the appropriate word.

We have already spoken (see page 14) of the prime importance of a reading knowledge. Since some may think that to put a foreign language into good English is, anyway, beyond the powers of most sixteen-year olds, it would seem a good plan to have two Unseen passages in future examinations—one for translation, and one longer piece on which questions in French would be asked. Such a compromise should satisfy those who have relied on translation in past years, and those who have relied on Direct methods and deplore having to relinquish them in the examination year.

(ii) *Translation from English*

However good the teaching has been in previous years, a substantial amount of revision will now be necessary. We all have our ideas as to what should be specially stressed, and how. I recommend having an exercise book prepared in which (left) a principle of grammar or syntax is stated, and (right) an example of that principle:

Il demeurait à Nantes, port célèbre	omit *un*, *une*, between two nouns in apposition

When some sixty of these have been recorded, one may proceed to prose extracts. These may be done together on the blackboard, by individuals in books, or round the class orally.

The average prose extract is usually a dismal affair—and often as not, an assemblage of phrases, or a totally meaningless extract. Examining boards should achieve a little human interest—say, *via* a story, or an abridged extract from a well-known book.

If the group is 'setted,' containing a fair number of those who may afterwards specialize in Modern languages, we may try to put a little polish on the translation. For example, we can try to avoid undue repetition. In French, pupils can make lists of synonyms or near-synonyms of the commoner words (in French: *aller, dire, donner, finir, très, le livre*, etc.) so as to ring suitable changes. French certainly seems to offer an embarrassing selection of synonyms, *vide* the equivalents for 'fat,' 'work,' etc., and, at the same time a certain poverty: *grand* for 'tall' and 'famous').

We have already spoken of Grammar in Action (page 34), *i.e.*, seeing grammar at work in a passage of the foreign language. One can now, in French, read to the class, say, stories by Maupassant, noting phrases helpful to style (*si c'eût été vrai; mon père, furieux, répondit*, etc.).

At this level, however, accuracy is paramount. The knowledge of grammar and syntax is deemed so important that the passage of translation from English is often an artful grouping of special sentences, rather than an example of the work of a gifted writer. (This will not do at higher levels, where suitable pieces—say, about the people and customs connected with the language—can be an education in themselves.)

In this translation business, one again feels sympathy for teachers who, for four years, have avoided the use of

English. However, their pupils—intelligent as they almost certainly are—should not be unduly inconvenienced. There will be ample time for the oral work on which they thrive; and, if proceeding to the sixth form, will have, sooner or later, to translate.

(iii) *Composition*

It is probably easier to write an essay in a foreign language than a translation: the subject and the form are one's own. Yet, at the same time, the free composition is the supreme test of ability. As such, it deserves an important place in the first examination. For various reasons, however, it does not always secure this. Some examining boards grant the essay a very small percentage because it does not lend itself to standardization: it may also be that pupils are liable to learn passages by heart for use 'on the day.' The examiners can, of course, detect the practice when a number of candidates use the same passage in essays of differing subjects, for example, a description of springtime in the country in compositions so variously titled as "A Day in the life of a Stockbroker," "Christmas," or "A Film you Have Seen." There is, of course, nothing harmful in the process, yet (like coaching for intelligence tests) it prevents the testing of true ability.

A compromise is furnished by the Reproduction. Here a story is read by the examiner, which is then reproduced with the aid of a plan. There is then less possibility of introducing pre-digested material about springtime.

Whatever sort of essay is finally written, the following principles may prove to be of value:

(*a*) Some idiomatic material, some sixty or seventy phrases maybe, should be learned, for possible incorporation. Let them be useful, everyday phrases, *je ferai de mon mieux*, or *er braucht eine Stunde, dahin zu kommen*, and not outlandish items such as *il y a quelque anguille sous roche*. They should have been freely used in practice essays, and disallowed if irrelevant.

(*b*) If, during the year, the maximum use has been made of the foreign language, the essay will be markedly improved. All sorts of conversational phrases can be included, and an instinctive feeling for the right expression, and the right word order, will be forthcoming. Anyone who has said, several times during the year, *je ne l'ai pas fait* or *wir haben es nicht machen können* will be several degrees nearer to perfection.

(*c*) As few pupils at this stage can handle a dictionary with confidence ('he paid his bill' = *il paya son bec*), suitable vocabularies should be given in the case of *free* composition. This will greatly help to build up a knowledge of the language. The words supplied will be of a technical nature, *e.g.*, terms associated with camping, or ships, wireless or films; thereafter, the essay-writer must train himself to seek synonyms for the words he does not know: on no account, should he entirely *rely* on the teacher's aids. Improvisation is, however, an exhausting business for less able people who, to write adequately, need a familiar vocabulary and a spacious plan.

(iv) *Dictation*

Many pupils find French dictations something of a problem. The nature of the language, a completely different set of vowels, lack of phonetic training, and bad pronunciation habits—all these induce a general feeling of helplessness. Nor is there much evidence that, with very poor pupils, a great deal can be done in the examination year. With most examining bodies, a count of over 20 mistakes means o for this particular question; I have had worthy colleagues, believers in weekly dictation, who have rejoiced when Higgins or Bulpington have brought down their mistakes from forty-five to twenty-five—and all without tangible result.

Apart from dictation practice in the certificate year itself, much can be done by regular practice in earlier years; by insistence on careful pronunciation (pupils who for years have been pronouncing *porté* and *portait* in the same way can hardly be expected to write them correctly in a dictation); and by a helpful approach on the part of the dictator, who should vary his technique to accord with the mood and ability of the class. He should not lunge about when reading: nor should he broach a new passage before everyone is looking up, having finished the last one.

Without incurring the labour of dictating whole passages, one can sometimes give short tests in which a single word, exemplifying a rule, has to be written; for instance:

(a) *il y resta UNE DEMI-HEURE* (*demi* invariable before the noun).

(b) *elle ne croyait pas qu'il FÛT malade* (Subjunctive for Past Historic).

(c) *des images REPRÉSENTANT une série d'accidents* (gerund, invariable).

(d) *un FRANÇAIS parlant anglais* (capital letters for the person, with words of nationality).

(e) *des chapeaux BLEU-CLAIR* (invariable 'double-barrelled' adjectives of colour).

(f) *deux CENT quatre-VINGTS soldats furent tués* (eccentricities of *cent*, *vingt*).

Equally well, one can stage a spelling test involving certain awkward words, *grand-mère, porte-plumes, intéressant, beaucoup, plusieurs*, etc.

But undoubtedly the chief difficulties arise with the e and ε verb endings—admittedly, when listening to Frenchmen, it is hard to detect much difference. However, pupils can learn to associate each sound with a particular lip-formation. Their notes are as follows:

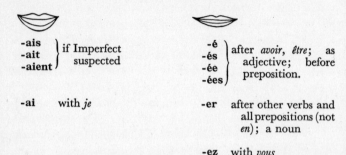

-**ais**
-**ait** } if Imperfect
-**aient** } suspected

-**ai** with *je*

-**é**
-**és** } after *avoir*, *être*; as
-**ée** } adjective; before
-**ées** } preposition.

-**er** after other verbs and all prepositions (not *en*); a noun

-**ez** with *vous*

This scheme, of course, presupposes that the rules are known concerning agreement of the past participle. These, too, may need 'working-up' in sentences such as *elle est retournée, j'ai tué ma bonne, la bonne que j'ai tuée, je l'ai tuée, nous nous sommes amusés, elle s'est brûlé le doigt.*

(v) *Oral Work*

We have already stated that speaking and understanding should be one of our highest priorities: and the course, till now, will have largely been geared to that purpose. The chief means of securing oral fluency are, no doubt:

(*a*) Making lapses into English as rare as possible.
(*b*) Describing pictures—this is a difficult technique, and it is probably best, having announced what the picture represents, to move methodically round it, commenting on left, background, right, centre, foreground in that order. The description should not be a mere list of objects; each noun should have a description as well (*ich sehe auch ein schönes Mädchen, das am Fenster steht*); and repetition should be avoided (by

means of pre-digested synonyms such as *il y a,
je vois, on peut voir, nous remarquons,* etc.).

(c) Continuation of the *Carnet moderne (Unterhaltungsheft).* See page 60.

(d) *"Lecture expliquée"*: where a long passage is
involved, a member of the class may be asked
in advance to summarize a section, and questions can be asked on the remainder.

(Let care be exercised with accent and
intonation during the reading.)

(e) Activities, such as General Knowledge questions
(set by one team to another), impromptu talks,
etc.

During the oral examination itself, it is sound practice
to give as long an answer as possible when questioned, using
pronouns for nouns, and avoiding bald replies beginning
with *denn, porque, parce que.*

(vi) *Foreign Studies*

In Chapter I (page 11), I claimed that modern language
teaching ought to 'open a window on to the world.'
There will be some who admit the truth of this at sixth
form level, but cannot see how it can be achieved any
earlier. "To bring a class of thirty or more to a level of
reasonable efficiency using only five lessons weekly, is a
superhuman task," they will object; adding, that if any
of this time is taken from them, they will not be answerable
for the consequences.

However, I maintain that even five years of French,
German or Spanish without any knowledge of the respec-
tive peoples represents a waste of opportunity: for if the
language lesson cannot break down an international
barrier or two, which lesson can? Ask any educational
inspector or administrator why modern languages have
been introduced into secondary modern schools, and the

F

chances are that this will be among his reasons. Surely it is also valid for grammar schools?

I ventured the opinion that, in grammar schools, where French is taken in public examinations, we ought, at the very least, to find time to throw some light on *France*. It may be done in the following ways:

(a) Personal Reminiscences—in most cases, these will be soon exhausted, and in any case are somewhat unsystematic.

(b) Wall-pictures (see page 25).

(c) Suitable courses.

(d) Talks or lectures by visitors (admittedly uncertain, and hard to secure).

(e) Pictures for description (see page 80).

(f) Notes given to people going abroad (see page 134).

Perhaps the best way, combining language with local colour, is:

(g) Through vocabulary:

Let us assume that a knowledge of French education, politics, empire, industry, agriculture, entertainments, transport, history and geography is essential to the understanding of France. (If, say, the history or geography teacher speaks French, so much the better—and another blow for the integrated curriculum is struck.) Around the following word list, what an entertaining commentary on Education can be woven!

cap	la casquette, le béret	
shorts	la culotte	pictorial repre-
plus-fours	la culotte de golf	sentation of
satchel	le cartable	school-child

primary school	l'école
primary scholar	l'écolier, l'écolière
secondary school	le collège, le lycée
secondary scholar	le collégien, la collégienne
	le lycéen, la lycéenne

in the	{ 6th form { 1st form	en	{ première { sixième

{ entrance exam. { Certificate of Education	le certificat d'études le baccalauréat

{ teaching { private study	l'enseignement (m.) les études (f.)

{ boarding school { day school { religious school	l'internat (m.) l'externat (m.) le collège (libre)

{ head master	le proviseur (lycée); le principal; le directeur
second master	le censeur (lycée)
head mistress	la directrice
master	l'instituteur (elem.) le professeur (sec.)
mistress	la maîtresse (elem.) le professeur (sec.)
bursar	l'économe (m.)
janitor	le concierge
usher	le surveillant

{ refectory { dormitory { class-room { study { playground	le réfectoire le dortoir la salle de classe la salle d'études la cour

{ break { return to school	la récréation la rentrée

{ to be put in detention	être collé, retenu	
to rag	chahuter	
to expel	expulser	
to go in for }	passer, subir }	
to pass in } an exam.	réussir à }	un examen
to fail in }	échouer à }	

{ day off { long 'vac'	le congé les grandes vacances

{ society { education, new type	le club les classes nouvelles

I will not encroach on space by giving any further lists, save to mention that the Continental scene is swiftly changing, and may require comment by the French or German assistant (if any), notably on politics; and that, when preparing word-lists, we must keep an eye on the type of vocabulary—often somewhat literary—favoured by Examining Boards.

Other word-lists (trees, animals, professions, etc.) are worth giving also, though they hardly enter the 'local colour' category.

Ideally, of course, a combination of all the above methods should be sought. The principle of Local Colour is already accepted in the number of excellent courses now on the market: it needs to be followed up. The vocabulary method does so, and has the advantage that boys and girls of moderate ability can derive from it something positive in the sphere of language. One day, perhaps, the importance of Foreign Studies will be recognized by questions in Ordinary and Advanced level papers. Their introduction will notably freshen the Ordinary level year, which many find so tedious.

There is one *caveat* to be entered. Teachers describing Roman and Greek life are presumably able to do so without political or personal prejudice. It is less easy to talk objectively of present-day France, Germany, and Spain. One teacher may remember the events leading up to Mers-el-Kebir; another will have been bombed by the Luftwaffe; a third actively disapproves of General Franco. Foreign Studies are only just beginning; but they must not become a medium for propaganda. In present-day Russia, it seems, English books contain some amazing details about ourselves—notably, that teachers beat their pupils unmercifully. Fortunately for the latter, however, they are often too poor to go to school!

(vii) *Alternative Papers*

(*a*) Language

Many examining bodies have recognized that certain pupils simply have not the intelligence to cope with the 'Ordinary' paper as at present constituted. Yet, so long as all candidates do the same paper, a further reduction in standards will make it farcical for the better people.

Translating into English, the duller pupils can muster enough vocabulary to produce something which, on investigation, bears a certain resemblance to the foreign text and also to the mother tongue; but they cannot retain any abstract principles, nor put them into practice, so that translation from English and free composition becomes a matter of appalling difficulty.

There are in existence a number of 'Alternative Lower Papers' offering an easier range of questions, that the less intelligent can get their teeth into—though the standard of marking is normally adjusted. Such variants are: Questions in English on an Unseen piece, instead of Unseen translation; questions in French on an Unseen piece, instead of an essay; and an Easier Prose. There is much to be said for all these; for, if oral work gets its due recognition—and 'C' type pupils often excel in oral work, which is a matter of temperament as well as of ability—we are in a fair way to stressing reading and speaking, the two most useful elements in language teaching. As regards Prose, if the year is not to become an unspeakable grind, the passage for translation should be an easy one, stiffly marked, rather than a highly technical piece that has to be leniently dealt with. Even so, an easy piece does not always give the relatively good linguist a chance to display his style. Thus, the weaker candidate, if he is to do Prose, needs his own easier piece.

(*b*) Language with Institutions

> "Je sortissait du— quand un voix, qui je savait trés bien, criat 'Savez vous cela ma femme avez ecris a vous trois lettres et n'a recevu pas une response?' "
> "Non je ne sait pas."
> "Eh bien, elle desire cela vous écrivez une lettre pour disez quoi vous faites."

S——, the author of this gem of French prose, at the time aged eighteen, was by no means incompetent at other subjects; indeed, he hoped to proceed to a University Diploma in Agriculture. Soon after recording the above, however, he failed Ordinary Level French for the fourth time. The loss to the nation's food supply might have been serious, had not the University suddenly waived its entrance requirements. (Some, incidentally, are suggesting that this should be widely done in the case of all would-be scientists who cannot learn a language.)

S—— was one of many boys in our grammar and independent schools, whose many years of French caused frustration to himself, his teachers, his parents and his four examiners (who never earned their fee lightly, since S—— always answered every question fully). An examiner myself, I can state that the number of boys and girls who have nothing to show for five years of French is increasing. Only a marked lowering of examination standards in any given year can fully conceal the problem of S—— and his fellows.

Had S—— passed at the fourth attempt, it would have been hailed as a triumph of 'guts' and pertinacity; his gratitude to the staff would have been immense; but it would have been a moral and not an educational triumph. However, he 'ploughed,' as do so many thousands of others, so that even this consolation was denied him.

Every school with enough boys and girls like S——

should offer a course in 'Language with Institutions' instead of the usual French or German or Spanish.

In England, we are firmly wedded to public examinations; jobs still depend on 'five passes'; and there are many critics of what has been called 'the Lambeth way to education.' The course I propose could, therefore, be tested by the university boards at Ordinary Level. It will not be leniently marked, and a 'pass' should satisfy the requirements of universities and professional bodies, as well as future employers. Incidentally, the General Certificate of Education was not meant to be a school-leaving examination; but so it has become, and in this respect bears a remarkable likeness to the old School Certificate.

After three years of a five-year course (though some would no doubt defer selection for one more year), or in the last year of a four-year course, we should be fully aware of those who cannot become modern linguists in the sixth form. Forming a group somewhat larger than the average bottom set (instead of the usual tiny company, whose only hope is its smallness) and thus reducing the size of other sets, they will concentrate on:

(a) Readings in the foreign language.
(b) Conversational work.
(c) Occasional reproduction of work read or anecdotes heard, and perhaps some letters.
(d) Foreign Institutions.

At this stage there seems little point in laying down a special syllabus for Foreign Institutions. If they are accepted, it will be easy to formulate a programme. Should French be the language in question, a book would be needed that described, in English, France and the French, not without reference to the European background. In one or two weekly lessons there might be scope for projects; for broadcast lessons; for the compilation of cuttings and pictures concerning French technical developments, French sport, French entertainers, etc.

News items, stories read, wall pictures, film strips, and occasional experiences will each yield information which can be co-ordinated under subject headings by a skilful teacher. A news-item concerning the dearness of food, calling for a note on French farming methods, will add to our knowledge on agriculture; a pupil, having described a film about the Moulin Rouge, will elicit a note on customs, establishing the fact that not every Frenchman lives in a whirl of desperate gaiety; pictures of the Tour de France will illustrate some Anglo-French differences in sport and psychology.

S—— would enjoy this: he could never break down the Relative Pronoun, but he might break down some of his own insularity.

When I have written about 'Language with Institutions' in the past,[1] it is this aspect that has been best received; though some correspondents suggested more oral work, and others, the reading of French classics in English (which I think a mistake; surely the answer is, simplified French classics in French). One practical correspondent hoped that, if weaker candidates were withdrawn from the main language papers, the examiners would not, as some of them now do, fail fifty per cent of the remainder.

If and when a course of this kind comes to be seriously considered, there will be many scoffers. "Soft option!" they will cry; or "Dilution!" Such people, I venture to think, will possess only a nodding acquaintance with Upper Five C.

---

[1] *e.g.*, in *The Times Educational Supplement*, June 4, 1953.

Chapter Five

THE SIXTH FORM

1. PROBLEMS OF ORGANIZATION

I WAS once present at a conference organized by an Institute of Education. The idea was to promote fellow-feeling between local school and university staffs, to familiarize each with the other's problems in the sphere of modern languages. As the afternoon wore on, however, the gulf between the two parties widened. The requirements of the professor and his assistants became more and more exacting: the teachers more and more conscious that they were not, apparently, doing their duty. The former wanted students who wrote accurately, talked fluently, possessed a flair for literary criticism, and an unrivalled knowledge of foreign institutions; the latter thought that one or two of these aptitudes was hard to find in a sixth-former, let alone a combination of all four.

The difficulties facing sixth-form teachers of modern languages are indeed considerable. 'Higher school' candidates, future university entrants even, are often taught with those content to 'keep languages alive'; certain smaller schools find the second language a forbidden luxury; others direct their brighter Arts pupils into the classical side; others, again, through the claims of science, have virtually no Arts Sixth, and the preparation of examination candidates may be largely a matter of private study and encroachment on the teacher's spare time; finally, in many schools, there is no money available for sending pupils abroad.

None the less, the sixth forms continue to produce many potentially good linguists; and this chapter, assuming reasonable conditions and the existence, if not segregation, of three separate types of pupil, 'Advanced,' 'Scholarship,' and 'Non-Specialist,' makes a number of suggestions for the improvement of this vital work.

2. 'ADVANCED' AND 'SCHOLARSHIP' CANDIDATES

(i) *Selection*

There is no reason why ordinary, hard-working pupils should not attempt a modern language at the old Intermediate standard; but to those anxious to specialize, to attempt scholarships and degrees, a word of warning should be given. Outside teaching, there are few specifically linguistic jobs; and there is no evidence that Arts graduates in large numbers will always be absorbed into industry, the Civil Service, and professions such as journalism and advertising. A prominent industrialist, Sir Frederick Handley Page, has revealed his disgust that fifty to sixty per cent of all university students are taking Arts courses: and Arts teachers have more than once been urged to persuade their ablest people to study science. It is pleasant to find that our capacity for self-denial is so widely recognized.

(ii) *Aims*

To a certain extent, both here and in other European countries, modern languages have usurped the place of the classics. Therefore they should provide a training which is no less efficient. The classical education was held to be the ideal one for six reasons:

> (*a*) It created an orderly mind, one able to master principles, and to put them into practice. (Such a mind was finely equipped to produce, in due

course, balance-sheets, Civil Service memoranda, administrative decisions: traditionally, the Oxford 'first' in classics made the ideal Under-Secretary or business executive.)

(b) It sharpened one's power of expression in the mother-tongue. Translation into English, esteemed for its accuracy rather than for its style, stresses the *mot juste*; and in translating from English, the very inadequacy of the classical language demands careful paraphrasing, and a purge of 'woolly' and redundant expressions.

(c) It encouraged literary criticism. To read great authors was to understand the mechanics of style (and incidentally to improve one's own).

(d) The study of Roman and Greek history—preferably in English, to avoid the labour of translation—linked the rise and fall of powers with man's own qualities and was thus a lesson in Ethics.

(e) It showed the influence of Roman and Greek Institutions upon our own, notably in the sphere of politics, law, architecture.

(f) Latin was the passport to other languages (the 'Romance' group).

Clearly, if modern languages cannot do for us what the classics did, or claimed to do, they deserve the same accusations of 'other-worldliness' to which Latin and Greek have been subjected.[1] Of course, there is a very real risk that the sixth-form language course, by attempting too much, may achieve too little—such, at any rate, will be the objection of those whose classes are unintelligent or easy-going. But the first five aims are those which

[1] *cf.* C. E. M. Joad, *The Book of Joad*, Ch. 1.

should be constantly before us, especially where certain of the sixth form are aiming at an Arts degree.

A course in French and German provides, of course, a passport to most other European languages, save those in the Slavonic group; though even here, the study of the German inflected noun will have given useful experience.

Broadly speaking, the first two aims will be realized via language; the third, via literature; the fourth and fifth, via other means which may be new to some readers.

(iii) *Language*

(*a*) Translation into English

Presumably because style is hard to define, few examining bodies are prepared to give high marks for it; in their reports, they sometimes comment on 'stylistic renderings,' but these are of little interest to them save against a background of accuracy. There is a flamboyant type of pupil who confuses style with fancy; any connection between his translation and the Unseen is largely coincidental. He has to be reminded, by means of the red pencil, that he is a translator, and not an author.

In our comments on Unseens at Ordinary Level, we referred to the practice of learning word-lists, and at the higher level, this practice can hardly be avoided. The examining boards often set for translation highly literary pieces, where difficult words stand closely together, making deduction well-nigh impossible. Personally, I do not set Unseens until we have worked through and learned about four hundred unguessable words. (This provides an opportunity to give a few etymological notes, showing how French, for example, has derived words from Classical and Vulgar Latin, Germanic and Celtic tongues, Italian, Spanish, English, etc.) Some examples are supplied, to avoid false translations back into French; thus, under D we have *dru* (*blé, pluie—pousser, tomber dru*) and under O, *obus* (*explosif*). Private reading, to enrich one's French–English vocabulary, is also confusing unless words are noted in their context. *Abîmer* (to spoil) might well turn up again in an essay—*je n'abîme jamais mes fils*.

To give some idea of my French list, here are the words beginning with *n*:

la nacre (nacré)
  naguère, erstwhile (*adj.*)
        but lately (*adv.*)
le nain
  nanti de
  narquois
la natte
le navet

la navette (en navette)
  navré
le nénuphar
  niais
les nippes (*f.*)
le niveau
le noyau
la nuque

During subsequent class readings, the list may be added to: and the English–French word-list used for conversation (see page 103) affords useful duplication.

Now that there is a good word-stock, we may venture some aids, in the shape of Major Points and Minor Points. We have touched on the matter in the Upper Fifth (see page 72). Such aids will, I think, be found to hold good for most schoolroom languages:

Major points:

  A. A few words may appear untranslatable if the literal meaning is to be preserved; translate them freely, putting the literal meaning as a footnote.

  B. Have a proper regard for the intentions of the author (*e.g.*, use of metaphor, length of sentence, choice of vocabulary, mood of speakers, etc.). Otherwise, it is a case of *Traduttore-Traditore*.

C. Undue repetition of words and sounds must be avoided (though this is, of course, a *sine qua non* of any English writing). An inelegant passage cannot be a translation of an elegant one.

D. Flexibility of words and clauses should be sought. A common example is furnished by the position of adverbs and adverb clauses. English often places these between subject and verb (he very frequently got up); German has a fondness for the initial adverb; French distributes the adverb quite impartially; occasionally, it even appears, to confound us, between subject and verb. Generally, however, we should be guided by the foreign word-order, which normally represents the author's sequence of thought.

E. In the stress of translation, faults of English are often committed of which the writer would not normally be guilty. Among these are a profusion of 'its,' 'hes' and 'theys' apparently unrelated to any noun; and badly-placed relative clauses ('the two dogs belonging to my Aunt, whose appetite for bones was insatiable'). There is no reason why *la clarté française* should not be matched by English clarity.

Minor points:

F. Parts of speech may be altered, *e.g.*, *der kalte Puritanismus* ('Puritanical coldness'); *la noire immensité* ('the immense blackness').

G. The English sentence is less able to dispense with the verb than is, say, French, *e.g.*, *nul bruit* (there was no noise).

H. In translating conversation, one should try to put oneself in the speaker's place: What would have he said in the circumstances?

1. Paragraphs may be re-arranged to achieve special effects.

I can only hope that these suggestions will have the effect of improving many an Unseen translation. When a satisfactory standard has been reached, it is important not to lower it by too much impromptu translating, *e.g.*, of set books, in class. We have spoken (see page 73) of classroom English, and there is no doubt that it is insidious in its effects. In calling for a quick translation, it is best to remind one's hearers that it is a Grade 2 effort, a hybrid, an unfortunate phenomenon, a test of comprehension and nothing more.

If we are wise, we must admit that certain passages do not lend themselves to translation, at any rate without factual inaccuracy. In that case, the footnote method is probably best. It has been said that only bishops improve with translation: proverbs, similes, and metaphors often defy us; over and above this, an 'atmosphere' is sometimes impossible to reproduce. Many reputable translators, in the supposed interest of readability, have wandered absurdly far from the original: a sixth form will often be interested to compare a set book and its published 'translation.'

Our old enemy, the book of disconnected Unseens, or set of examination papers, remains to be dealt with. As we have already noted (page 73), the ideal book would provide, with each Unseen, a note on the author, his background, and his style (use of words, effects achieved by punctuation, division into paragraphs, etc.). Unfortunately, for obvious reasons, obscure passages are often set—sometimes, one feels, because they bristle with rare words—and these would lend themselves less well to analysis. But we must try to link all aspects of modern language study, language, literature, history, etc.; otherwise,

we shall have water-tight compartments within subjects which themselves, to a dangerous extent, represent
water-tight compartments.

The practice of translation into English (at least, at
sixth-form level, where more than mere accuracy is looked
for), can greatly strengthen our powers of expression, of
that I am sure: we learn to vary our language, to weigh
our words, to avoid what is ugly or ambiguous. A pupil
who writes an English essay offers something more dis-
cursive than an Unseen: one simply cannot read it all
critically. But if he is to earn our praise on a short passage,
he will not only have appreciated the author's talent, but
will also have exercised his own.

(*b*) Translation from English

Not many items of grammar and syntax should remain
to be discussed in the sixth form. (The further collection
of vocabulary is dealt with under *Oral Work*, page 103).
Formal Grammar lessons, therefore, may not be required
—at any rate with abler classes; and new constructions,
such as the concessive clauses in French (*si jolie qu'elle
soit*, . . .) and some of the more refined 'if' clauses in
German (*hätte er daran gedacht*, . . .) may be covered
during the very process of translation. When returning
a Prose, I ask the class to open a special exercise book;
a double page is headed according to the title of the Prose.
We write (left) new or half-forgotten points of grammar
and syntax; idioms and vocabulary are inserted (right).
In working new Proses, notably in German, we use a
similar technique: this time, we put our communal
translation on the right page, where a system of numbers
and letters refers us to the grammar points and derived
vocabulary on the left page. All this can be tested
periodically.

There remains the question of style, particularly in

French, which is usually begun earlier than German and Spanish, and where there is less satisfaction to be derived from a translation that is merely accurate. On which author should we base our style? The question is perhaps academic before the scholarship year. A more immediate query is perhaps this: Does any objective criterion of style exist? My own view is that there are certain absolute values such as variety, euphony, and balance: and more important still, clarity and conciseness. Our masters are therefore Voltaire and Flaubert rather than Rousseau and Balzac. The search for effect—elegance, suspense, eloquence, and so forth—hardly concerns us yet; and, in any case, is more relevant to free composition.

Variety

We have tried, at the Ordinary Level (see page 76), to secure variety of language: the list of alternatives to common words should now be extended. A circle reminds the writer of repetitiveness; he is already familiar with the T (wrong tense), G (gender), and the following underlinings:

        _____ Error of grammar or syntax.
        ========= *Mot juste* required.
        ~~~~~~~~~ Wrong construction, inaccurate paraphrase, etc.

Under the heading of 'variety' comes the selection and use of 'Idioms.' These can, of course, be dictated, but it is far more instructive to secure them via class reading, notably of short stories by worth-while nineteenth- and twentieth-century writers. One can use these as *lecture expliquée*, noting idioms the while, or give them a Grade 2 translation, adding new words to the French–English or German–English list.

    Idioms and interesting *tournures* or effects can sometimes be obtained from private reading. 'Read widely, pencil in hand' was advice formerly given to me, but, in my opinion, it only has limited application for the average sixth-former. He has insufficient time when his set books or general literary reading is done; he may not read sufficiently fast for enjoyment; he is not discriminating enough, and therefore does not know what he should take down.

Learning by heart a passage for subsequent reproduction does supply variety to a free composition, but its value for prose translation is slight. It is apt, too, to be forgotten when required. With re-translation, a portion of the foreign language is put into English (left page), and after a delay of at least three or four days, is rendered into the foreign language (right page) and compared with the original. There are, however, various drawbacks in this process. The rendering into English must be rather literal, and may thus infringe the rules of good translation. One can, in places, write a more or less stylish English translation, with the literal translation following in a bracket: *elle eut un geste de dédain*, 'she made (had) a gesture of scorn.' The foreign language page will need, however, to be scrutinized by the teacher, for certain of the pupil's phrases may well be correct, though not identical with the original.

Euphony, Balance, Clarity, Conciseness

An ordinary reading lesson, or study of a set book, may easily yield better examples than those I have given below, and, indeed, other principles:

Euphony

A. Avoid repetition of harsh sounds (*une histoire qu'aucun lecteur ne croit*).
B. Avoid hiatus (*un étudiant éveillé et laborieux*).

Balance

A. Arrange predicates in ascending order of length (*passons| en revue| les doctrines religieuses*; or *nous entrâmes| dans la maison| vers sept heures et demie du matin*). It is, of course, better to break up a 'mass' of predicates: *chaque dimanche* nous allions faire *notre tour de jetée en grande tenue*. The last predicate should be at least as significant as the others, or bathos results.

B. The subject, if considerably longer than the verb, should follow it (*au moment où commence notre histoire*; or *voilà ce que pense le jeune homme aux cheveux blonds*).

Clarity

A. Adverb clauses are often movable to the head of the sentence, or nearer the verb (*de sa vie, le duc n'avait jamais entendu une telle histoire*). A final *de sa vie* would be somewhat ambiguous.

B. The sentence must be complete in meaning— completed, perhaps, by a personal pronoun (il va à Londres, j'*y* vais rarement); by a reflexive pronoun (la porte *s'*ouvre); by *que* (il dit que c'était vrai, et *que* je m'étais trompé—the second *que* showing *assertion*, not *fact*).

C. The choice of past tenses often gives extraordinary clarity; *e.g.*, the *Perfect*, describing a recent occurrence, or a state of affairs still going on (il partit: on ne l'a pas revu depuis); or the *Imperfect*, to show habitual action or to 'pin-point' a dramatic development (je lui donnai un pourboire: stupéfaites, mes sœurs me regardaient).

On the score of clarity, two things may be said: French must be precise, where the English is vague (*ils avançaient d'un pas grave*, 'they walked gravely') or metaphorical (*rien ne frappa son regard*, not *rien ne frappa son œil*). Again, word order should not, in the interests of clarity, be needlessly changed when translating, for the original author, in arranging words and clauses, had certain intentions; yet correct order, in a non-inflected language, is an essential. Other things being equal, Subject-Verb-Object is a good basic order for the translator.

Conciseness

Normally, a French sentence is shorter than its English counterpart: we should, therefore, avoid rambling sentences, endlessly linked by *et* or relative pronouns, and aim for short sentences, representing each a single idea and a single breath. Some suggestions:

A. Avoid dead wood (*personne ne parle autant que NE LE FAIT mon frère*).

B. Use participles (*arrivé là, il rebroussa chemin*, instead of *quand il fut arrivé*).

C. Use infinitives (*il croit avoir raison* instead of *il croit qu'il a raison*).

D. Use Ablative Absolutes (*son voyage terminé, il retourne en France*).

There are many other procedures—changing parts of speech (*je préfère son exclusion* = 'I prefer him to be excluded'); reflexive verbs (*il se fâche* = *il devient fâché*); verb omission (*rien de plus simple; nul bruit*); adjectives replacing clauses (*furieux, il me regarda* = *il fut furieux et me regarda*); parenthesis (*cela est sain, paraît-il* = *il paraît que . . .*).

The value of prose translation is considerable: it too makes for an orderly mind; it greatly facilitates one's power of expression, by stressing certain universal criteria of style, and discrimination in the reading of a text as well as in the choice of words. If the Classics demand skill in paraphrasing, where words such as 'patriotism' have no exact equivalent, modern languages often require selection between a number of *apparent* synonyms.

If a well-educated foreign assistant is on hand to help with the selection, so much the better.

(c) Free Composition

Obviously, all we have said about style is applicable to free composition: for some, alas!, composition is little more than translation.

On completion, the essay should be re-read with the same attention as for prose-translation: re-read, for its effect on mind (variety of language, clarity, conciseness) and ear (balance, euphony). It is a good plan to read aloud, if the environment permits.

Content cannot be without importance, and some few minutes should be devoted to a preliminary plan.

A specialized vocabulary is best given when the essay title is chosen, and this is sometimes 'married' with the conversation lesson (see page 103).

(d) Oral Work

It is not easy to keep the language alive in the sixth form. Paper work reigns supreme; the accent is on translation; the use of the foreign language in class, therefore, is liable to seem incongruous. In the main, it is perhaps best to limit oral work to specific times or periods.

It must be admitted that there is little external stimulus to oral work at this level. Even where the total is compounded of oral *and* written marks, the proportion of the former is usually a small one—thirty out of three hundred and seventy, for example, or forty out of four hundred.

The same disregard for oral fluency is liable to continue throughout the degree course, save where residence abroad for three or six months is a condition of securing a B.A. Where this is not so, *e.g.*, at our more conservative universities, the graduate's knowledge is often the reverse of practical. An examiner in oral French and German at the Civil Service examination (Administrative Grade) assures me that the worst work is often done by Modern Language candidates from these universities.

If the 'A' and 'S' level test is of ordinary conversation, one can prepare for it in various ways. At 'O' level we used Question and Answer (under subject headings); *lecture expliquée*; Picture Descriptions. To these may now be added such features as Debates; News Talks; and the lecture on Foreign Institutions, followed by question and answer (see page 111). Sometimes an acrostic is useful. In the game known to my own family, for various reasons, as Emu, one takes a word such as SET, and arranging it as below, inserts letters to form French and German words:

S	érieusemen	T		S	at	T
E	xist	E		E	ich	E
T	anière	S		T	reue	S

These are then defined; the setter obtains two points if his word is not guessed within a minute; the guesser one point. The umpire, deciding if the definition is adequate or no, may refuse the two points.

If any member of the sixth form proposes to become a teacher, he or she can get useful oral practice by helping to instruct a junior form.

But all this is building bricks without straw, unless there is a methodical attempt to build up vocabulary. The *Carnet moderne* or *Unterhaltungsheft* has begun the process; in the sixth form, the weekly or periodical conversation lesson will continue it. It is no bad plan to begin each lesson with a word list, writing English words, and calling for their foreign equivalents. Additional exercise is given if the words are then defined. Titles of word lists can be chosen to suit all tastes: School, Army, Navy, Air Force, Theatre, Cars, Post Office, Sport, etc.; Adverbs; Adjectives; Daily Actions. By these means a wide vocabulary—frequently tested!—is assembled. Two further references are made to the current list: a free composition bearing upon it can be set, and a talk given the following week. The sixth-former chosen to talk will be expected to show ingenuity by using as many of the words as possible.

Preparation of such lists is also invaluable in the sphere of translation from English. It is astonishing how quite able pupils are stumped by fairly common words. A further safeguard is provided by reading to the class a piece of English prose, preferably something bearing upon the foreign country, listing unknown words or phrases, and learning their equivalents. (A possible title: Words That Escaped Our Vigilance.)

Modern languages, with their double discipline, would seem to go further than the Classics. When we write, or say (with first-class accent), *das hätte ich nie gedacht*, we have absorbed a *principle*, and put it into *practice* in two ways, like musicians playing the same air on piano and violin. It is a matter then, not only of the orderly *mind*, but of orderly *organs of speech*.

(e) Dictation

There is not much to add to our remarks on Dictation in Chapter Four; however, our class is presumably smaller now, and there is an opportunity of understanding more fully the principles involved. First, as time for Dictation is often limited, it may be well to concentrate on the technical points in a given passage, without wasting time on straightforward sections. Thus, a dictation might consist not of a connected passage, but of a series of sentences such as *je ne pouvais nier qu'il FÛT venu; sie wünschte nicht, dass er ihnen vergäbe*. At the close, there will be time for a discussion of errors. Why did it have to be *vergäbe* and not *vergebe*? Or, to test aural precision, one can walk round the class and take a list of errors. Pupils are then asked to pronounce the correct sound followed by their version of it, *consommé—consomé, Veilchen—Veilschen*, and so forth.

It is possible that thousands of man-hours per month are spent in dictating to English boys and girls, without a full appreciation of the utility of the task. Surely there are two useful operations: the ear must register the sound, and thus there is aural training; the mind causes the sound to be transcribed. In *je ne pouvais nier qu'il fût venu*, the ear rejects *fou*, presenting us with *fus, fut* or *fût*; the mind, putting principle into practice, selects *fût*. Among those who can reason, the dictation cultivates an orderly mind; it also aids the discriminating ear. Aspiring musicians, as they pore over their dictations on a hot afternoon, may find their task lightened by this assurance.

(iv) *Literature*

The study of literature is now firmly established at sixth-form level, and there is widespread agreement that, as a background to language, as a study in national thought and writing techniques, it has considerable value.

Of late, however, there has been a tendency to attempt too much in this sphere. Where General Literature has replaced Set Books—although it may only be required of Scholarship candidates proceeding to a university, while Set Books can be offered by Advanced candidates, it is often, for reasons of convenience, taken by the whole group—teachers having to do, often with inadequate resources, what formerly fell to university staffs.

Incidentally, in this and other matters, teachers do not have the freedom and independence that most professions look on as a right. University examiners, as they read the literary answers of sixth-formers, cannot fail to ask themselves whether official demands are too exacting.

There has been a tendency, in recent General Literature papers, for Criticism and Appreciation to supersede one or two of the general literary essays. Though this is a step on the right lines, it does not mitigate the evil: candidates are glad to have fewer questions to answer, but cannot well specialize—say, in the seventeenth and nineteenth centuries in French Literature, or read one or two authors only of the seventeenth, eighteenth, and nineteenth centuries. These studies cannot be done in isolation.

It would probably be better to use the old Set Book system for *all* candidates, insisting that one or more be offered from each period. Each answer should relate the author to other authors in the same *genre*, preceding and following: it should place the author against a historical and social background, and also call for personal judgement. Thus the set book would, once more, become the focus of study. To try and cover several hundreds of years in General Literature, without plan or syllabus, is too vague altogether, at this stage. Furthermore, it bewilders and exhausts the slower pupil, and encourages hasty and haphazard reading; whereas success in Unseen passages demands exact comprehension. General Literature, if it is done at all in school, should be left to the third or scholarship year. To embark on it prematurely is to encourage intellectual dishonesty—the issue of cyclostyled notes, the meaningless generalization, the too frequent recourse to Lanson or Robertson, followed by a shameless regurgitation of other people's opinions.

Even a longish essay on a Set Book—merely to translate a passage from it is hardly testing enough at this stage—presents difficult problems. Teachers themselves are rarely competent to relate literature to history, sociology, economics, music and art. Owing to the demands of language, literary time is often short. Books, written especially for sixth-formers, and stimulating their thought-processes, are conspicuously few.

However, to make the best of the present situation, we will first see what constitutes the ideal literary essay, and how it can be produced:

(*a*) It should be planned, from notes assembled in advance.

(*b*) It should look forward, backward, and sideways, *i.e.*, a social critique of *Le Mariage de Figaro* should have regard, both to *Le Bourgeois Gentilhomme* and to *Le Gendre de M. Poirier*, as well as to similar themes, say in English or German.

(*c*) Literary trends should be related to those, say, in art, architecture, and music, and illustrate the social, political, and religious background. (In the absence of good textbooks, this would involve some dictation of notes—see also page 111.) Obviously this favours the candidate with a wide general knowledge and a resourceful mind, rather than the earnest pupil who is happiest when 'swotting up' single topics.

(*d*) There should be some quotation.

Here are some ways in which the ideal essay may be achieved:

A. The works of the principal authors, *e.g.*, (in French) Corneille, Racine, Molière, Voltaire, Beaumarchais, Hugo, Vigny, Musset, Balzac, should be on hand and extracts, affording comparison, read in class. The latest critiques should be available in the Library.

B. The maximum use should be made of information

other than that supplied by books—wireless talks and play performances, film strips, films, talks given by members of organizations such as the Alliance Française; perhaps a speaker from a local university would assist, or the local branch of the Modern Language Association.

c. Members of the class who also study English will be able to secure practice in literary criticism; and the additional chance to write essays will help them to marshal their ideas. (English is an excellent accompaniment to modern language studies.) The class should be urged to read theatre, film, and book criticism in periodicals, and to listen to wireless critics. (It is because so many class notes will be in English that one must regretfully admit that English is, for this purpose, the best medium of writing.)

d. Class time should be given for discussion of style, philosophy, personal opinions, etc. Therefore, the ideal set book is one which does not require the whole lesson for translation—in other words, where language is not a barrier to literature. Why *Romeo und Julia auf dem Dorfe* pleased me, becomes a more rewarding question than what that long-winded critic in the Library says about it. (Sixth-formers accustomed to displaying their own views will have little trouble with Passages for Criticism and Appreciation.)

Next let us examine the task of Criticism and Appreciation itself. The sixth-former, confronted with a piece of prose or poetry, is required to disengage its theme, to comment upon form, style, the emergent personality and special technique of the author and, when requisite, upon versification. He may also be asked to assess literary value and to assign the author to a particular school or period.

Frankly, I should not like to have been set such a task at eighteen, and I doubt whether many candidates of this age succeed in giving evidence of genuine critical power.

Apart from the critics who figure in most school libraries, there are a number of books giving guidance on the matter. But though they can tell you what to look for in a given passage, they cannot stimulate your reactions or emotions. There are, therefore, the following disadvantages:

(a) Candidates that are emotionally immature, or without critical power, will tend to say what they think they ought to say (or what Faguet says), rather than what they feel impelled to say. This is artificial, even dishonest. (Such candidates are probably the least able linguistically, and thus suffer the additional handicap of imperfect understanding of the passage.)

(b) Other candidates, who cannot admire the apparently admirable, feel frustrated, and adopt a mood of cynicism.

However, this type of work has apparently come to stay, and if the literary values of a small minority are encouraged, something has been gained. The following suggestions may, therefore, have some value; but it is stressed that the candidate must already be a person of some discrimination:

A. There should be as much integration as possible with the rest of the Literature course. This is easy if Set Books are studied, and intensive study of texts results; if General Literature is followed, texts should be used, rather than dictated notes, to exemplify, say, the style of Flaubert. (It is, of course, expensive to provide sets of supplementary readers, but there are now on the market a number of cheap, paper-covered editions published in France.) The 'marriage' of Criticism and Appreciation with Set Books would heighten, of course, the value of the latter, especially where practice passages are taken from the Books themselves. Similarly, a passage of Criticism and Appreciation is more manageable if it has been taken as an 'Unseen' in a language lesson.

B. Where a passage set for Appreciation is completely self-contained, *e.g.*, a sonnet by a previously unencountered poet, it is well to give some information on the author, his motives and habits. This should interest and educate. The study of a series of unconnected extracts may be as monotonous as the familiar book of mixed passages for Unseen translation.

On the whole, it seems safe to say that prose extracts will make a wider appeal than poetry to the majority of eighteen-year-olds, notably boys. The enjoyment of poetry, despite the efforts of C.E.M.A. and the B.B.C., is still for the minority. Courses of music appreciation in schools have not vastly improved the musical taste of the nation; and it may, alas!, be a fallacy to assume that taking authors to pieces increases our affection for them.

There remain three things to be said. Firstly, vast tracts of General Literature, excessive numbers of set books—both are harmful to detailed and thoughtful study. As the Arts sixth-former frequently offers French *plus* one other modern language *plus* English *plus* Latin, it seems wise to limit the number of set books to four per modern language; or, at the most, five. Sometimes, six are set, with the proviso that one or two shall be studied privately. It is doubtful whether the average sixth-former has enough verbal knowledge or *savoir-faire* to do the latter efficiently.

Secondly, what of the moral aspect of literature? Examining boards generally offer quite a handsome variety of set books, and some think that in making our choice, we should be moved by moral considerations. It seems to me that we should be neither too prudish nor too sordid, neither too obsessed, for example, with Romanticism, nor with Realism. A year with Corneille, Lamartine and Musset would seem too divorced from reality; a year with *Candide*, *Le Mariage de Figaro* and Maupassant's *Contes* too depressing. We should, I think, seek for variety, observing that the sensuality or pessimism of an author stems from his life or times, and has not necessarily any value or relevance for normal people under present conditions.

Thirdly, where the same candidate is liable to be reading French, German, and English, teachers responsible will find that co-ordination will lighten both their own and their pupil's loads. There should, in fact, be regular meetings of those concerned. A sixth-form career should not begin with the simultaneous study of Shakespeare, Goethe and Verlaine.

To sum up: the Literature course should awaken the critical faculty, but over and above this, it should afford practice in good writing, and also trace the development of ideas and experiences, nationally and universally. One might say that classical authors were first on the scene, but that subsequent writers have been able to take the human story a stage further.

(v) *Foreign Studies*

Many people would agree that some knowledge of foreign institutions is an essential part of higher language study; but how to accommodate it is another matter. All of the following aids I have, at one time or another, found useful:

(*a*) Modern Language Club. This will not only afford practice in speaking foreign languages, but can also be harnessed to the special needs of the time, *e.g.*, the discussion of Western European unity.

(*b*) Scrapbooks. These are made from 'hand-outs' from current Western European magazines.

Headings are suggested which classify foreign customs and institutions. (See also pp. 26, 88.)

(c) Background Books—though I admit that concise, arresting and up-to-date works, especially in German, are hard to find.

(d) Lectures from visiting speakers or assistants, arranged by the local M.L.A.; or suitable courses staged by the W.E.A.

(e) Foreign Films, at commercial cinemas or Film Society shows. Some of these are, frankly, less educational than others.

(f) Essays. We have here a certain link with language. In French, we might take the following topics for a two-year course: *L'Histoire jusqu'à la Fin du 17e Siècle*; *le 18e Siècle*; *le 19e Siècle et après*; *La Politique*; *L'Education*; *L'Empire*; *Le Caractère Français*; *Les Régions de la France*; *La France et son Economie*; *La France et le Monde actuel*; *Sciences*; *Musique*, etc. On these subjects one can give a forty-minute talk in French; the class will take notes (practising what it may have to do, some years later, at the university); these notes are subsequently reproduced in essay form. There should be time for questions; the class may be impressed more by differences than by similarities, and if it feels that French, German and Spanish are the languages of decadent peoples, the causes (which would not be unconnected with love of comfort, failure to reproduce, militarism or religious obscurantism), should be understood. The ethical content of the sixth-form programme is not always high, but most subjects can do something to fill the breach.

(vi) *University Scholarships*

Conditions vary so widely that it is hard to say anything of general application; but the following points may safely be made:

(a) Translation into English of prose and poetry will need to be more ambitious. The intention of the author, as expressed in his order and choice of words, punctuation, paragraphing, etc., must be better understood and reproduced than previously.

(b) Translation from English and Free Composition will necessitate the learning of fresh material, *e.g.*, idiom, descriptive phrases, linking clauses, particularly those that aid in the development of an idea, 'on the other hand,' 'some think that,' etc. A grammar fault should be a rarity. One should be able to imitate, for particular reasons, the style of particular authors. The teacher must take care, when giving Model Answers, to explain clearly the *nuance* of every ill-chosen word.

(c) Essays on Literature, History and Institutions—not every good linguist, alas! excels in this field—call for wide reading, notably of literary texts and biographies; a good English prose style; liveliness and originality as well as hard work; an integrated picture of the Western World going back to the end of the Middle Ages, with history, society, and literature closely inter-related.

(d) Oral work (accent and fluency) must be above reproach: at least one stay abroad should have been made. This is, no doubt, asking for the moon; and open awards are, at the moment, no less difficult of attainment.

3. NON-SPECIALISTS

In many grammar schools, a spirit of extreme materialism prevails. Examinations are the gateway to a job, and, therefore, what is not examined is scarcely worthy of consideration. So it is not remarkable that sixth-formers 'having their French maintained'—it is usually the language of Bossuet and Voltaire which is thus prostituted —often do so under protest or with resignation. However, a well-planned course, whose advantages have been carefully pointed out, may do something to inure them to their lot.

Seekers of open scholarships will, of course, try to maintain their skill in Unseens, which are often set during this ordeal. They cannot, in one or two weekly periods of their third year, be expected to master long lists of words, but should be trained to use their deductive powers, and to admit that gaps in their translations represent sheer timidity. (For the art of translating, see pages 92–6.)

SCIENCE students are usefully occupied in the following activities: beginning German or Russian; producing a work-book of translations from scientific periodicals, or from books of scientific and technical extracts, choosing themes of particular interest and appending illustrations; reading, in a simple form of the foreign language, books on foreign institutions; reading general texts, notably of the twentieth century; or doing an occasional 'snap' translation from English, *e.g.*, of an item in the current day's newspaper.

ECONOMICS students would be equally well suited, save that for scientific periodicals and text-books, economic articles from a French daily, and books of economic extracts would be substituted. A course on so-called commercial French could also be useful.

H

Students of ENGLISH, HISTORY, and CLASSICS might also begin German or Spanish; should have a working knowledge of French institutions, and read, not only twentieth-century texts, but works in French dovetailing with periods or themes in which they are specially interested.

All these groups should be trying to maintain their conversational powers.

Sometimes, groups of sixth-formers are mixed, and appeal may be made to their natural interests; research can be carried out in the library, and handbooks of French scientists, authors, musicians or painters produced.

Writers of school text-books have tended to concentrate on works that prepare for examinations, and those "brushing-up" their French have been ill served. There is scope here for a first-class illustrated course for the sixth-former who has passed his last language examination; also, he deserves, but rarely gets, an enthusiastic teacher. It is a sad commentary on our ways that this important cultural work is so often neglected. There is no doubt that more and more of our able sixth-formers will be going into industry and commerce. Modern languages may not only be valuable there, but will also represent an aspect of that general knowledge which, we are told, is so often lacking. When scientists are made to pass an Arts subject at Advanced Level, and Arts sixth-formers must do the same in Science, a blow for liberalism will have been struck.

Chapter Six

SECONDARY MODERN SCHOOLS

I MUST begin this chapter by admitting that I have never taught in Secondary Modern schools.

I have, however, come into contact with them on various occasions. From that experience, from the place these schools occupy in the educational world, and by extension of my remarks about the grammar school 'proletariat,' it is possible to draw some general conclusions. Such conclusions may not be without value, in view of the hopes expressed by Mr R. Birley and others, that a vast extension of language teaching can powerfully influence world relations.

Let me record three visits to Secondary Modern schools, each of which helped to form my opinions on the problem.

One hot day in a southern county, I was brought to a classroom where forty-five boys of twelve or so sat rigidly to attention. Called by name, they rose, one after the other, to recite the various parts of various tenses of various verbs. This occupied a complete period, one of three given weekly. As a modern language lesson, in this particular sphere, it was as impressive as it was valueless. Dr Johnson might have said of it: "Sir, it is not well done; but the wonder is, that it is done at all."

On another occasion I attended a French lesson, given to an equal number of boys, and held, late in the day, in a dark, old classroom of an industrial town. This time, a story was being read, and questions asked upon it. The material was congenial, and the lesson could have been a useful one. Unfortunately the class was in an uproar, despite the fact that a number of ringleaders had been brought out to the front, and bidden to sit on the floor. "We can't get a decent teacher," my host said, as we went out. "This fellow has a history degree. We had to press him to take French."

Soon after, at an Open Day, I watched the girls of a third school perform a French playlet. It was well rehearsed, and well spoken. None of the performers, perhaps, would ever use the French she had so painstakingly learned, but they had all had a pleasurable experience, and some might conceivably be impelled to continue it at an evening institute.

These experiences confirmed my belief that language teaching in Secondary Modern schools must be done by trained teachers on unorthodox lines or not at all. True, there is no such creature as a Secondary Modern 'type'; through a local shortage of grammar school places, a number of relatively able people, more intelligent than those formerly consigned to central schools, may well be found in Modern schools. In the main, however, it must be true that the pupils of such schools suffer precisely, and more acutely, from the disabilities we have noted on page 66. I view with horror, therefore, any proposal to subject them to academic discipline—to foist upon them grammatical abstractions, literary language, a passive rôle. I have already seen enough bored and listless children in grammar school classes. Fear of punishment, and of failure in examinations, kept their boredom within bounds. Such motivations—to use a fashionable word—would be far less powerful in the Modern school.

Yet, as I write, it is proposed to secure one of these incentives by the public examination. Unless this, too, is of an unorthodox type, the excellent work of many pioneers will have been wasted, and we shall have a race of frustrated children whose contribution to international friendship will be nil.

1. PRINCIPLES

Basically, the aims should be those set out on page 87, the priorities being reading, conversation, reproduction, and foreign institutions; the ways and means, essentially those upon pages 66–7. In the Modern school setting, these will be our principles:

(i) *Repetition*

If the course were highly selective, Modern schools in certain areas could learn languages by the accepted methods. It seems that prognosis tests of linguistic fitness are, as yet, far from reliable: but children who read, spell, and write English accurately, who have deductive power and a head for abstractions, will probably reach a fair standard. For administrative reasons, however, an entire 'stream' or year may be set to learn a language. These will not construct sentences *via* the application of principles, but rather when use of all the ingredients of that sentence has become automatic. Wishing to say "I am called Rose," they will be hopelessly slow in assembling *je m'appelle* from a knowledge of the Infinitive and of the rule for verbs containing a mute ə. I notice that Miss Evelyn Coulson, in her excellent *French in the Secondary School*, spends the whole of the first lesson in getting forty children each to say *je m'appelle*. In 1944, certain well-wishers of Modern schools were wont to say that their pupils, academically weak, would have a countervailing skill in crafts. Few people now claim that Modern school pupils will quickly learn a language, even by repetitive methods. On the contrary, they will keep on superimposing their English and subsequently, in the same situation, may well begin, *je suis appellé*. But it will mainly be by repetition of a relatively small number of words and phrases that they progress. For the expenditure of much time, there will be little to show. But by working from principles—admirable though this process may be —there will be even less. It may be taken for granted that, by basing sentence construction on grammatical principles, we shall kill all hope of spontaneous reactions. *Je suis froid* will drive out *j'ai froid*: a kind of linguistic Gresham's Law.

(ii) *The Teacher's Technique*

As I have already said, the less intelligent child has to be encouraged. In the modern language lesson, this will be particularly essential, since the subject has formerly been considered too hard for most pupils. Yet all the teacher's kind persuasiveness will be wasted if he has not, at the same time, a reserve of firmness. There may be large classes: there will certainly be a great deal of oral work, which will not absorb all the class's physical energy. We shall dwell later upon Variety and Activity, but the basis of it all is the gifted teacher—that man or woman most likely—alas!—to be tempted into the grammar school by better pupils, allowances, and a quieter life. Such a teacher will need a degree, which allows him to study modern foreign institutions as opposed, say, to history of language; which requires a stiff oral test; and a period of residence abroad. To keep him or her in the Modern school, we need a more flexible salary system, whereby successful pioneering work in such schools may receive some reward. It is doubtful whether we can entirely rely, for this important task, on the products of Training Colleges. In any case, it is worth graduate status. Further, when secondary school expansion has slackened, there ought to be sufficient graduates available. The physical excellence of many Modern schools, as much as their reputation, should help to inure many graduates to their new rôle; and a period of training there will give them an understanding of the Modern school mind.

The teacher will need vigour, patience, firmness, presence of mind. He may have to fight for his subject. He must be ready to exchange ideas with others doing the same work. He will, in short, be a quite exceptional person.

(iii) *Value*

As with grammatical principles, so with studies as a whole: they are unlikely to commend themselves even to the average child unless they have some link with day-to-day life and language. It will, therefore, be a sound principle to emphasize the situations that he will experience, the life and adventures that he would enjoy, if he were a youthful Frenchman or Spaniard.

The ideal teacher, as we have seen, will have travelled: the ideal book will afford a picture, neither glamorized nor caricatured, of the foreign country, artfully stressing similarities and differences. The course as a whole will strive to incite curiosity, interest in foreign correspondence, travel, politics, sportsmen, and even entertainers, so that class time and leisure time are integrated.

A foreign *assistant* from the neighbouring grammar school should come and ask simple questions, and give short talks. He is the valuable end-product, like the bomber that wartime workers were often taken to see.

This knowledge of the foreign country will not be profound, and will be hard to test, if testing should be needed. But, for reasons that I shall adduce, it is well worth trying to put over.

It is nowadays fashionable to reply to children's questions as to why they are asked to do anything; in this case, the course itself will furnish the best answer.

2. NECESSARY CONDITIONS

Any teacher planning a Secondary Modern school course ought, I think, to try and secure the following *necessary conditions*:

(i) *The Daily Lesson*

A child learning his own language will be severely handicapped by long, inactive intervals. How much the more so a Modern school pupil who is in touch with a foreign language for only 40 minutes each day, in a crowded class, with no lesson between, say, Thursday and Monday, and no homework? True, his aims are limited, but the language teacher must press for the best possible timetable. Nor, after the first year or so, should there be any reduction in time. It is then that faster progress will be possible, when the class is reduced in size through transfers, or the disappearance of weaker elements.

(ii) *The Size of the Group*

My first experience of a language class in a Secondary Modern school was, as I have said, with a group of 45. Such a figure is absurdly large, for though in a predominantly oral course (in accordance with our priorities), there can be much chorus work, the individual must have the maximum experience of expressing his own thoughts. It therefore seems desirable that the language period should synchronize with a 'lecture' type of subject (history, social studies, etc.) or with a craft (if there is adequate space). The latter classes could be larger, to facilitate a smaller language group, and would receive pupils who, as time goes on, prove to lack linguistic ability. If this savours of special pleading for the language class, I can only reply that, if the job cannot be done properly, it should not be attempted at all.

(iii) *Integration*

Even a daily lesson will be a 'drop in the ocean' if there is no connection with other lessons. If French is studied, the language teacher should ask his colleagues to deal with French History and Geography: *The Scarlet Pimpernel* or *A Tale of Two Cities* might be read in English.[1] The local French 'assistant' can speak of social studies from the French angle. Projects, of course, form the best link between various lessons. Again, the unfortunate language teacher will be told that the entire school cannot rotate around himself. I assume, however, that in being given a difficult assignment, he will receive encouragement from head teacher and local authority.

(iv) *The Follow-up*

After three or four years the pupil's knowledge may be practical, but it will not be profound. Towards the end of the course, the Head of the local Evening Institute will be asked to talk to the class, and to encourage enrolment for the following September. The Secondary Modern child will have learned *via* special methods: and ideally, there should be an evening class, limited to him and his contemporaries, or catering for his special needs.

(v) *Basic Languages*

Whatever inspectors and pedagogues may say, it will surely be necessary to reduce the total volume of grammar and syntax—and even to condone the milder errors of speech and writing. There is, at the margin of most modern languages, a substantial field of useless rules that educated foreigners themselves ignore. There are also words and expressions useful to the foreigner, but which

---

[1] There are those who would try out the Classics in Secondary Modern schools—via translations, models, popular stories, film strips, etc.

may safely remain 'passive' with us. They can be 'touched on,' but it will not be necessary, in this sphere at least, to employ them. In offering too rich a diet, we shall cause indigestion: in being pernickety, we shall become tiresome. In a number of subjects, woodwork, English, singing, for example, we do not worry overmuch about perfection—and in modern languages, even in grammar schools, a knowledge of our own limitations is essential.

In FRENCH, the following items could well be 'passive':

A. *Tu* and its derivatives. The secondary modern child should be warned that he may hear this word in the bosom of a French family, together with a verb form which he will probably recognize, but that its use by him is unwarrantable. Strictly speaking, even the teacher can dispense with it when addressing children of 11 and over.

B. *Celui*, *le mien*, etc., which can be replaced by nouns.

C. The Past Historic (and, of course, the Subjunctive, together with various compound tenses). Even the Future (replaced by *je vais aller*), and the Perfect (*je viens d'aller*), can be almost indefinitely delayed. Many unlettered continentals, of course, notably in Spain and Italy, get along quite nicely on the Infinitive.

D. The Present Participle.

Errors to be condoned would include: *plus bon*; *il envoye*, *nous espèrons*; *nous sommes allé* (I have heard *elle a mouru* from the lips of a cultured Belgian); *le huit Septembre*; *la langue Française*; *des méchants garçons* (*des jeunes gens* is already showing the way); *il est un fermier*; *c'est difficile de comprendre cela* (and its various permutations); *il ouvre ses yeux* (a rule which, in view of its frequent disregard, is hopeless to defend); *six heures et demi*, etc.; *deux cents vingt*; *il a refusé venir*; *je vous veux partir*. Most of these could well be considered satisfactory, even at the grammar school level.

GERMAN, virile language that it is, easy to spell and pronounce, and spoken by people whose desire to exchange visits with ourselves can, seemingly, never be assuaged, could be popular in Secondary Modern schools. But before its introduction, something will have to be done about cases. I suggest a course which disregards the Accusative altogether: this will, of course, involve the horror of *ich will mein Vater besuchen*, but which is no more horrible, perhaps, than singing *ich sag's ihm grad' frei ins Gesicht*, or our own dialectical forms *give I that basket*, and the even more erratic ''er wouldn't come along o' we.' The Genitive, too, might be scrapped: here one would presumably replace *der Mann des Volks* by *der Mann von dem Volk*. I have even heard people urge the abandonment of the Dative, certain phrases involving this case after a preposition being learned as idioms as and when they arise.

As with French, *du* and its derivatives would be removed from the active list.

(vi) *The Book*

The all-important question of grammar having been dealt with, we will now consider those qualities which the aspiring teacher should seek when choosing a book. Some or all of the following features should be present:

    A. A separate volume per year—a recurring book is wearisome.

    B. Well-spaced print.

    C. Lively illustration—in colour, if possible; pictures illustrating stories; advertisements from foreign newspapers, etc.

D. Suggested activities: maps to draw, collections to make, games to play, etc.

E. Present-day vocabulary, introduced largely under topic headings, Food, Clothing, School, Sport, Wireless, etc.

F. A supplement with easy short stories for class or private reading, preferably with vocabulary on the same page.

G. General information (at outset or end) on history, geography, derivations of words, famous foreigners, travel, etc.

H. Short phonetic exercises, particularly in the first year, with pictures showing the shape of the mouth as for different vowels.

I. Exercises of a 'passive' sort—masculine to feminine, singular to plural, insertion of appropriate verb, brief plans of stories and reading matter for reproduction, orally and in writing, suggestions for dramatization: periodic revision exercises or tests.

J. Grammatical explanations brief, clear, as free as possible of abstract terms.

K. Suggestions for use of note-book. Since accuracy of both ear and eye is sought, new grammar and vocabulary will be copied down, or subsequent activities like dictation, reproduction, and correspondence will become impossible.

Finally, the book must secure orderly progress, and sufficient variety to "break up" the year's work.

One objection may be made: could such a course be used by those who may be transferring at 13+ or later to the grammar school? In my view, to try to cater for both needs will be to meet neither. The children likely to mature late must have special coaching in the

Modern school, or, better still, on arrival in the grammar school. There cannot be too much liaison between such schools.

3. EXAMINATIONS

Certain politicians, justifiably anxious for the future of the Secondary Modern school, have been urging its adoption of the G.C.E. This, they think, would give it a higher standing among parents, pupils, and public. Others think that an examination would give the pupil confidence, encourage further study, and even stimulate the staff! These well-meaning people do not always envisage the examination in its *present* form. In some form or other, however, a public examination seems certain to come: how, therefore, could it assist the modern language course?

It will, firstly, be unreal to expect of the sixteen-year-old Modern School language pupil, competence in prose translation and free composition. For years he will have done only a modest amount of written work: his errors, in the interest of fluency, will have been treated with gentleness: he may not have enjoyed a daily period: probably he has done no homework, for (to quote a recent speech-day address):

"Most of you do a certain amount of evening work, and I am in favour of boys earning their pocket-money; but you simply must not turn up in the mornings late and dull and tired."

Into what examination system should the Modern School pupil be drawn? First, there is the G.C.E. Some have called for three levels—Advanced, Ordinary, and Lower; but I should still deplore the imposition, on the Modern school, of university-sponsored tests.

Secondly, there is the College of Preceptors, which provides for fifteen-year-olds in independent schools, where the stress is very much on academic discipline. One wonders whether this is quite the *milieu* for the Modern school.

As I write, the Associated Examining Board is to set papers of differing types in existing subjects, and to introduce new papers, mainly of a technical sort; but, judged by its syllabus, the prospective break from tradition appears too mild to accommodate Modern school children (though its high mark for oral work is welcome).

Whichever organization ultimately does the job, it must not regard the Modern school as a pale imitation of the grammar school. In French, it should produce a paper to accord with the Modern school priorities (which are closely akin to those of weaker pupils in grammar schools). The following types of questions might suit all tastes and also permit some variety in teaching methods:

(*a*) Choose *one* of the following passages, and answer the questions in English (a far worthier exercise than one involving translation into English).

(*b*) Study the following pictures. Then, by using the word-patterns provided, write a short description in French.

(*c*) Write short notes on six of the following: General de Gaulle; Joan of Arc; the French Riviera; Indo-China; the French *lycée*; Maurice Chevalier; Renault; Louis Bobet; Pasteur; Chopin; the Tour Eiffel.

Finally, it is widely claimed that the present Ordinary Level is too hard for many grammar school pupils. Yet to simplify it further is to make it farcical for cleverer pupils, and to whittle down standards: the hundreds of poor scripts that I, as an Examiner, mark annually, would then become the norm. The Modern School needs a course of its own, and therefore—if it is to be so burdened —an examination of its own. If this had anything in common with present Ordinary Level papers, it would reinforce, among Modern School pupils, the sense of failure that is, we are told, their chief handicap.

4. THE EFFECT ON INTERNATIONAL RELATIONS

What, next, of the view that a vast increase in language learning will greatly further international relations—or, to set a more limited aim, European unity? I personally believe in an extension of language studies (by unorthodox methods, and under proper conditions) for entirely different reasons: I cannot think that the advent of 'languages for all' will hasten the millennium.

Firstly, while large classes are the rule, both at home and abroad—even thirty being a Utopian figure— linguistic attainment, and knowledge of other countries, is likely to be small.

Secondly, international friendship is too often at the mercy of politics and economics, and alas! of the psychology of rulers.

Thirdly, international planning, whereunder, say, a committee of nations would assign to each a number of languages to be learned (*e.g.*, Britain might be 'zoned' for French, German, Danish, Spanish, Russian) is likely to be hampered by questions of prestige. A plan for Europe, unless it is to be merely political, must have regard to the Russians, who are sensitive on cultural matters. *Le Monde bilingue*, according to which educated Europeans should learn English and French as well as their own languages, is a most sensible conception, but it enrages the Germans.

Fourthly, a vast increase of overland travel, which is the obvious way of putting precept into practice, does not yet appear physically possible: but if, under some latter-day *Kraft durch Freude* organization, great liners brought thousands of tourists to the main European ports, what irritations might result! After all, the inhabitants of pleasant suburban avenues are not notably delighted when droves of trippers appear, dropping paper into the front garden, and peering over the wall.

To my mind, the essential reason for widening the scope of language teaching is the breaking-down of isolation; or, as we have said elsewhere, opening a window on to the world. For children who spend almost a lifetime in a small industrial town, (with a week each year at Blackness), the escape from an environment, the exercise of an imagination—these are surely worth-while experiences. Since there is no magical teaching method, Secondary Modern French may not always be good French: the thrill and triumph of speaking another language may not endure: there may not be the same financial incentive to learn as obtains in many European countries. But the wider outlook that we hope to secure through language teaching—this is, perhaps, the best answer to those who would crowd it out with more English or more Mathematics, simply because these are the stuff of everyday life.

Chapter Seven

FOREIGN CONTACTS

IN all modesty, I should now like to study the question of foreign correspondence and foreign visits: I realize, of course, that the amount of experience I have gained is pathetically small, compared with the sum total of wisdom whereby, each year, thousands of British children exchange letters and visits with their counterparts on the Continent.

Let me say, at the outset, how strongly I believe that what we remember of our school studies is what we find practical use for; and children derive great satisfaction in discovering such value, becoming twice as teachable thereafter. Furthermore, foreign contacts accord with our two aims: firstly, of providing a 'window on to the world'; secondly, of giving a strong priority to oral work.

I do not pretend that all children speak fluently after four weeks in another home; I certainly do not claim that occasional letters lead to automatic mastery of the Disjunctive Pronoun: but I do believe that these activities cause pupils to think that "this is my subject," or even that "this at least is worthwhile."

There will be general disagreement with this; both on educational and social grounds. Continental teachers have several times told me that foreign visits, in particular, are educationally harmful, interesting their charges in agreeable and volatile activities, such as talking, and weaning them from the more worthwhile business of translating. Then there is the cynical view, expressed by the late Dr Joad, that the more we see and know of other people, the less we love them. I venture to disagree heartily with both these views. I feel that foreign contacts provide an enthusiasm spreading over the whole range of language work; and herewith record, that I cannot call to mind one case of strong personal antipathy in many hundreds of foreign exchanges. Young people will not treat their foreign counterparts as soul-mates: *camaraderie* may even wear thin; but, in the main, they are far more tolerant than we think.

Then there are critics who, while agreeing that foreign contacts enrich language teaching, point to the difficulties of putting precept into practice, particularly with visits: the personal expense for the teacher—despite the availability of leaders' tickets—since not every Local Authority or Head Teacher is able or willing to help; family problems; the need to escape, for a while, from the young; foreign teachers dilatory in matters of organization; general paper-work; and in the case of exchanges, long journeys, since not every British school can find a link with Western Germany or Northern France. Nor are teachers always honoured for their labours: French schoolmasters, I know, often find inspectors completely uninterested in their outside activities, though reserving the right to criticize their lessons in the most trenchant manner.

In making a number of suggestions, both for foreign visits and foreign exchanges, we will see whether some of these difficulties can be broken down. On the score of personal inconvenience, it can only be hoped that the results may compensate: on the question of expense, that the Local Authority or principal teacher will be far-seeing.

1. FOREIGN EXCHANGES

There is hardly any linguistic value in foreign *tours*, as opposed to foreign exchanges. They may have some

athletic purpose, for example, winter sports in Switzerland, or hockey matches in Germany; they may possess
cultural value, though most children are allergic to
monuments; they may afford a change of scene; but
they will not add materially to one's knowledge of a
language. Nobody should arrange one, unless he can
organize and control.

Foreign exchanges, on the other hand, are immensely
simpler for the leader, who has only to escort his people
to a foreign destination and return them in good condition; if he remains on the spot, he can visit various
families and will no doubt be suitably entertained;
if not, he can travel out, and then return to England,
going out again in time for the homeward journey: provided, of course, that the 'link' school is reasonably
near.

(i) *Selection*

The gloomy prophecies of Joad and others will fail if
care is taken in selection. Who should exchange? Firstly,
no one who has done less than three years of the language
concerned. I have had continentals in England who have
studied English for only one year, with the result that
their hosts have talked French or German at home and
abroad—not a very equitable arrangement. Conversation
is bound to take place in the language of the stronger
partner, if there is marked intellectual disparity. Secondly,
only those temperamentally able to "have a go." Who
would learn a language, must first be prepared to maltreat
it. Quite moderate pupils without inhibitions are often
successful abroad: furthermore, they often prove more
observant than their cleverer companions. The perfect
introvert (though a foreign exchange occasionally brings
him out), the person who is impossible to amuse or
entertain, the cautious type who will say nothing till he

has got his Accusative or his Personal Pronouns in proper focus—these should all remain at home.

Then the right people must be paired—intellectual with intellectual, athlete with athlete, and so on. No use sending a non-swimmer to stay at a lakeside resort with the local breast-stroke champion; a shy serious lad to the home of some beau who likes girls and dancing; the virile type to hob-nob with a 'weed'; the poor child to a wealthy home, from which he may return in a mood of discontent. It is usual to fill up forms, giving particulars of the prospective visitor; but, to be safe, I favour an additional summary which must be heeded by the other side: "Fat, jolly boy." "Good mixer; likes cycling." "Very keen and clever at languages." "Pretty, popular girl." "Mechanically minded." "Rather babyish."

(ii) *Duration*

Except in the case of really able people, I doubt whether a period abroad of less than three weeks is of much value. All of us, however gifted, take time to attune ourselves to another language; and during the first of the three weeks, one is merely groping. Naturally, if the language course in school has been realistic, one will get off to a quicker start. Holidays, of course, do not always allow of two periods of three and a half or four weeks each, but there is no reason why the party from Cologne or Rouen should not arrive in England before term ends, and get a glimpse of grammar-school life. Similarly, the foreigner often starts the autumn term earlier than we do, and English children are always interested to have a day or two at the German *Gymnasium* or the Belgian *Athénée*, or observe the rigours of a *lycée* refectory in France (Belgium, incidentally, represents good exchange country: French seems to be spoken more slowly there, though solecisms are sometimes heard).

(iii) *Integration with Classwork*

As we have said, when there has been, by all concerned, a reasonable amount of oral work during the year, the visitor becomes much more quickly acclimatized. However, there may be, among the party, some who find talking difficult. It is a good plan to give these some advance lessons in conversation. Short periods centred round such subjects as Shopping, Post Office, Meals, Sport, Describing the Home Town, may be relied on to prepare the visitor for actual situations. Such pupils may rest assured that if they are temperamentally fitted to go abroad, and do not object to rushing in where the genius fears to tread, they may well be among the successes of the party. The foreigner enjoys educating us, and in this he is but human.

On return, those who have become fluent may experience some dissatisfaction with the dry, academic nature of the course. The answer to this is that the course should not be dry or academic. There will be the maximum possible use of oral work: notably talks, by returning travellers, on the country concerned. Any slang that has been picked up will be treated with indulgence: though we must not go so far as M. Aristide Pujol, whose *Joyous Adventures* are so well described by W. J. Locke. Aristide's English girl pupils, it will be recalled, treated an august visitor to such colloquialisms as *eh ben, mon vieux, ça boulotte* (when asked how they were getting on); and *allons étrangler un perroquet* (Apache-wise, when inviting him to an after-class cup of cocoa).

(iv) *Local Colour*

We have already tried, via Wall Pictures (p. 25) and Scrap Books (pp. 26, 88, 110), special courses (page 85) and word lists (page 82) to break down insularity and to give an effective picture of foreign countries. Now is the chance to complete the picture. I do not think children should go abroad without a sheet of notes dealing briefly with Geography, History, Trade, Education, Customs, Politics, Family Life, Sport, National Characteristics, etc. Whilst away, they can note down their impressions—say, for inclusion in a School Magazine article. (As we have said, it is wise to be reserved on the question of 'Culture' —Music, Art, Architecture and so forth.) Nowadays similar notes are sometimes employed when troops are sent to countries of occupation, and efforts should be made to avoid the social *gaffes* which often occur in efforts of this kind. (Minor errors of *fact* are, however, usually cheerfully pointed out by our foreign friends.) Films, brochures and pictures provided by Continental railway companies can also be shown with advantage before, but not too long before, the visit begins.

(v) *Ambassadors of their Country*

We mentioned that the need to escape, for a while, from the ebullient young, might keep at home many would-be promoters of exchanges. This ebullience may be just as distressing to fellow-travellers as to foreign hosts, so that the visitors become very poor 'ambassadors' indeed. We all have our methods of restraining the young; and, for a list of things to be deprecated, it is only sufficient to read the letters annually addressed to *The Times Educational Supplement* at the close of the summer holidays. Thus, on August 21, 1953, we find a lady teacher complaining that someone had allowed his boys to leave their railway carriage, in order to molest her girls, and bar their access to the *toilette*. On September 4, 1953, a correspondent wrote about two teachers who, staying with their children in hotels or hostels, went out shortly after their arrival, leaving their party unsupervised during the evening. Another group was led by a teacher on his honeymoon, who, not unnaturally, disappeared whenever he had a chance. (It was an unorthodox honeymoon, no doubt, but perhaps it was that or none at all.)

There is, in all these letters, a consensus of opinion that such teachers are also poor representatives: as are those who speak the operative language badly, or not at all.

Whatever travel organization be chosen, whatever country selected, there is no doubt that block exchanges are the least fatiguing and the most productive of all foreign contacts. Even where fluency has not resulted, there is an experience, and a mental picture, that make the exchange one of the most rewarding of all activities. One can only sympathize with children and students behind the Iron Curtain, who, as I write, may not have the privilege: at least, as far as Western countries are concerned. Despite all the minor injuries, losses of luggage, missed trains, and anxious parents, I have enjoyed them, and feel reasonably sure that much ignorance has been broken down, and many misunderstandings avoided.

2. OTHER VISITS

I should be presumptuous in offering advice on **Foreign Tours,** though some of what we have said under (iii), (iv), and (v) is applicable. Clearly, the best counsellor will be the manager of the local tourist agency. **Treasure Hunts** are well spoken of by those who have organized them: a boy or girl is given an itinerary, a bicycle, and a limited sum of money. The hunter, to prove he has fulfilled his missions, must secure information at the towns along his route—the name of the stationmaster at Gerolstein, details of church history at Evreux, etc. Having only five pounds or so, he must also do odd jobs in exchange for board. Then there are **Cultural Exchanges,** whereby, say, a boy in Birmingham, knowing no German, exchanges with a Düsseldorf boy whose English is good. This is excellent for international understanding (obviously Secondary Modern Schools, where no languages are taught, could participate), and valuable for general knowledge, though some might think it benefited the other fellow's export drive. Yet, until more English schools learn German, it remains the best hope for improving Anglo-German understanding. **Academic Exchanges** (you spend a whole year in my grammar school, I put in the same time at the Gymnasium) are not yet feasible on any large scale, nor ever will be, until education for international understanding receives the same priority as education for bread-and-butter (Economics for miners, daytime classes for young engineers, and so forth). There are **Summer Schools,** mainly for senior pupils, stressing aspects of national culture. The question of **Teacher Exchanges** merges into the general question: To what extent is the Government prepared to encourage teachers to understand and impart foreign cultures?—in the official view,[1] an essential task. At the present moment, official encouragement to students and teachers to go abroad, and to teachers for the exchange of classrooms, is distinctly meagre. In fact, a colleague of mine, who taught for a year in Austria, dipped heavily into his capital in order to make ends meet: and he is not the first so to impoverish himself. Was the advantage to him alone? Another teacher known to me was allowed by his authority to take up a teaching post in France for one year, but only on condition that he retired at 61 instead of 60. In all these matters enterprise is hindered, mediocrity encouraged.

[1] *e.g.,* Mr D. Hardman, Parliamentary Secretary to the Ministry of Education, at a 1949 Western Union conference.

3. Correspondence

Who first hit on the idea of correspondence between schools? It was probably one of those administrators with the traditional disregard for the teacher's spare time, and for the chaotic habits of the young. Yet, despite enormous wastage, such schemes multiply. Writing letters to complete strangers is, obviously, a human foible. To further their knowledge of languages, and from an innate curiosity schoolchildren do it—in French, German, or whatever is at the moment being studied, not forgetting Latin[1]: so, too, do adults, in the languages of the evening institute—plus Esperanto. There are offices where you can buy addresses at a few pence a time. A popular daily recently made some 'amazing disclosures' of the purpose to which people were putting bureaux of this sort. For reasons only slightly more creditable, people write to film stars, wealthy legatees, and handsome boxers.

Foreign correspondence inspires children to greater effort, though it does not add greatly to their sum total of knowledge. We should encourage it, and, by following a few precepts, we can secure the maximum value from it without wearing ourselves out in the process:

(*a*) We should entrust correspondence only to those likely to continue it.

(*b*) We should, for the purpose of encouragement, devote a period in school to preparing the first letters.

(*c*) We should ensure that the participants correct each other's errors after writing their own letters:

Wrong	*Right*
Last week *I shall* be very ill.	Last week *I was* very ill.

(*d*) We should be ready to help with impromptu translations after hours.

[1] For an account of the Orbilian Society, see *The Times Educational Supplement* of August 22, 1952.

K

(*e*) We should ensure that the school to be corresponded with, and its teachers, are really interested, so that we are not for ever sending out 'hasteners.' It is idle to pretend that teachers in general are willing to spend hours piloting such schemes—as I myself realized, when suggesting recently in an educational newspaper, an interchange between British and Colonial schools.

(*f*) Correspondence should also be linked with foreign exchanges. It should precede the exchange, and may well follow it if the exchange has been satisfactory.

(*g*) Letters received should be frequently read aloud in class; notably by the possessor.

Despite all these suggestions, however, it is probable that no more than twenty per cent of a class which takes up correspondence with every sign of zeal will be still writing a year later. If they are, the letters will be both brief and naïve. Yet correspondence is a fertilizer, by the aid of which a sturdy plant sometimes grows.

We have suggested that children who speak no foreign language could well participate in exchanges—English being the medium of speech. There is no reason why Secondary Modern Schools in this country should not correspond with foreign countries, and a scheme has already been evolved, whereby the local grammar school interprets for them.[1] If pride does not stand in the way, this might very well be extended.

[1] See *The Times Educational Supplement*, December 28, 1951.

Chapter Eight

NIGHT SCHOOL

1. THE SET-UP

A PERSON who has not learned a language at secondary school, who wishes to reinforce a language already begun, or intends to begin another, can be educated in a variety of ways. There are correspondence courses; gramophone records; lessons in the Forces; Teach Yourself books; wireless instruction; private language schools; and classes in day and evening institutes (commercial, technical, literary and general). Most of the latter take place in the evening, and their venue is often colloquially known as 'night school.' Here, any language may be studied, and school leavers are to be found mixing with greybeards of 80 or more.

If environment had any effect on educational progress, we might discount these places altogether. I remember vividly my first appearance, many years ago, in one of the London County Council's night schools. The building, a great, grim, grimy three-storey barrack in a decaying north-eastern suburb, was unprepossessing enough. But the scene within was infinitely worse. Each floor had a central hall, where, in the daytime, children of the primary school assembled on their special occasions; from each hall radiated corridors that were dusty, ill-lit, and smelling strongly of disinfectant. These corridors led to cheerless rooms filled with tiny desks at which, each week from September to June, our students—not

infrequently men and women of generous proportions—
spent one, or possibly two, uncomfortable hours.

However, Adult Education rarely has a home of its
own; and I have seen men and women inspired in Nissen
huts, and in the alcoholic atmosphere of the Miners'
Welfare. Much more serious was the extraordinary range
of intelligence among my pupils. A class of 30 might
contain students who, in due course, would be taking
examinations of Higher School standard; others could
never grasp what a Direct Object was, or the particular
functions attaching to *ser* and *estar*. In common with
many others, as revealed by Lavers and Rowntree in
their symposium *English Life and Leisure*, I had sometimes
thought parsons to lead an easy life: I now see that the
capacity of their Sunday audiences is as varied as that
of my first L.C.C. class, so that the successful sermon
becomes a masterpiece. A beginners' class in French,
of course, would be more consistent: that is to say, con-
sistently poor, for few of its members would, in the usual
course, have attended a grammar school; but classes in
Spanish and German, being heterogeneous, might be
almost impossible to run without some form of sub-
division. I used to give some thought to the question
of entrance tests, and even produced some of my own:
they had value when there were sufficient beginners, say,
in German, to warrant three or four classes. Even then,
the delicate mechanism of 'setting' was disrupted by
Cupid, who wished to include in the same class Miss X
(I.Q. of 60) with Mr A (I.Q. of 120). (To exclude Miss
X altogether would have been educationally undesirable,
and politically impossible.) In the end, of course, the
duller students would leave of their own accord: though
Miss X might linger on, getting vicarious pleasure out of
Mr A's intellectual successes.

As the session wore on, the graph of class attendances

began to show a marked decline. I could not be blamed, I think; the decline was, and is, a well-known phenomenon in this type of education, and very little can be done to arrest it. Minor ailments, domestic upsets, winter courtships—all play their part, but more often it is a matter of sheer mental inadequacy. I usually found that, if a student had been absent once or twice, it was by no means easy to bring him back; if, by chance, he returned, he tended to need private tuition while the others gossiped. And it is, under most Authorities, woe to the unfortunate instructor whose numbers fall too low: his class will be telescoped with another, for economy's sake, and all his problems will begin afresh. (One of my Principals took a fiendish delight in rationalization: a year or two after, the whole institute closed.)

If the environment is sometimes depressing, and the quality of the class, save in higher grades, unsatisfactory, the calibre of the teacher may leave even more to be desired: for much of the work is done by part-timers for low fees—so low, indeed, that a London teachers' trade union has been formed; and at Scunthorpe, not long ago, part-time lecturers were forced to strike for higher pay. These part-timers, in my section, were mainly in business during the day time; the rest were professional teachers. Among the business folk, a number were Continentals. They may not have been versed in the principles of pedagogy, methodology, instructional technique, and so forth, but, if they had had experience— and some had been for twenty years or more in the business—they made extraordinarily good teachers, for they brought into those dingy classrooms the atmosphere of their own country.

I was a part-time teacher myself there, but I have to put on record that my colleagues who, by day, practised in school were less effective than the Continentals. Yet, surely teaching cannot be as specialized a business as this. I am certain that 'night school' represents an excellent change of experience, if teachers remember that the adult has to be cajoled rather than browbeaten, that he may not want to be forced into examinations, and is quick to resent any suggestion of superiority.

Having given this picture of part-time education, which may well depress both present ratepayers and future students, I must stress that my experiences were some of the most exhilarating I have ever known. Teaching adults is normally a pleasure, for, unlike some school-children, they are anxious to learn, and are sound critics of a teacher's skill. Their eagerness often stems from the consciousness of missed opportunities—though one Principal I knew, who spent his days among boys and girls, felt his students needed incentives, and would offer them dance tickets as a reward for regular attendance. Few of my students were there for bread-and-butter reasons, and, on the whole, they were an inspiration. We opened a modern language library: we went on tours: we organized societies and produced plays. (During the latter, the curtains all too frequently failed to open; finally, they would part, revealing a red-faced producer in braces and shirt-sleeves.)

Perhaps these few reminiscences will reveal, more clearly than cold facts, the difficulties that attach to teaching outside school. Yet we must always make it possible to begin a language at any time: the grammar school has no complete monopoly of useful brains, there are the changing needs of commerce, the sudden inspiration of leisure; and if small fees are to be charged, classes will rarely be select enough or homogeneous enough. Let us see, then, what we can save from the chaos, and what useful suggestions can be made.

2. SOME PRINCIPLES

(i) *Students' Requirements*

The motives of a class of, say, 25 beginners in French will be exceedingly mixed. Some hope to go abroad; some would like to be able to read novels and magazines; some intend to correspond with friends met on foreign holidays; some wish to rise in the commercial world. Others have no particular idea what they are there for.

Clearly, the first thing to do is to get these motives down on paper and plan accordingly. We need not worry unduly at the outset about commercial, or even technical requirements. Apart from the fact that commercial languages, unallied to business acumen, do not normally enrich the student, their study is not an end in itself, but rather a matter of superimposing vocabulary on sound grammatical knowledge. We are back, then, to the usual priorities of reading, speaking, and understanding; and unless examinations are contemplated—they are, of course, a useful incentive—there need be no more translation into English than is necessary to illustrate a difficult point. Most modern courses for adults bear this out, and include no translations among the early chapters.

As the years wear on, priorities may change; but the desirability remains, of knowing what the class is after, and getting it to agree on a general policy. If the group is numerous enough, it may of course be possible to divide it into two—'Study German' and 'German for Leisure.' As to method, almost everything we have recommended for younger people holds good—the maximum use of the language for class purposes, some phonetics (in French, at least), the organization of the lesson, and—last but not least—some local colour.

(ii) *Personal Relations*

In the day school, boys and girls are there, whether they like it or not. No doubt they need persuasion as well as coercion, though some say that boys are sycophants by nature, and admire the dominant type of teacher. But with older folk all, save the most zealous, need to be cajoled. Demands on their spare time are often pressing. Their memories of school are not always blissful ones. They have not always faith in their own powers. There may be no bread-and-butter incentive. The instructor, therefore, needs to develop an affinity with the adult student: if he is merely there 'for the money'—modest though it doubtless is—he is not likely to have much success. I should like to suggest how such affinities arise:

(*a*) The tutorial method. When a set of marked exercises is returned, it pays to have a private minute or two with weaker students. They may even, at the outset, be completely bemused by our manner of correcting.

(*b*) The postal method. This consists of a friendly post-card whenever a student is absent, and, on his return, a brief summary of last week's lesson. The officious Principal, to whom I have referred, used to write threatening cards to absent students, warning them that they would be 'fired' if they did not return. Small wonder that many stayed away.

(*c*) The social method. Contacts with students are made after hours, notably in a language club, in visits to foreign films, or, at the end of the session, in an outing, or at a dinner. If the institute has a class of English for Foreigners, these will often attend the language club, and impart a very authentic note.

(iii) *Planning Courses*

In an institute of any size, there will be 1st, 2nd, 3rd and 4th year classes in the main foreign languages (and possibly drama, commercial, and conversation classes as well). Any overall plan for, say, four years of German will obviously have to be flexible in the extreme. Its class having been closed, as an economy measure, one 1st year group may not have finished the first session; Mrs A may have enrolled for the 2nd year class because, though a virtual beginner, she cannot attend the 1st year class on a Tuesday. Under the most favourable conditions, much will have been forgotten between one session and another: therefore, there will have to be a considerable amount of revision at the start of each year. Like washing-up, it is tedious but necessary.

Sudden changes in demand may leave some instructors stranded and render others more sought after. In the 1930's, Hitler's 'registered marks,' only half the price of ordinary marks, filled the German classes with intending travellers. Any country that cares to devalue its currency can affect the demand for its language in British evening institutes. Late hours at the factory may also operate: on this account, I once altered the start of a German class from 6.30 to 7.30 P.M. It failed, not because of the change, but because people were tired at the later hour. But the instructor did not comprehend. *Das ist mein Brot und Butter,* she said sadly.

Chapter Nine

PAST, PRESENT, AND FUTURE

COSTLY suggestions for the reform of modern language teaching are unrealistic. We have to spend an increasing proportion of educational money on new schools and technical colleges, and modern language problems receive only occasional notice. Of the many reasons for urging higher expenditure on education, national prosperity is one of the most pressing: it cannot, alas, be proven that, by halving the size of language classes, we should immediately lower the cost of production or stimulate our exports.

For from urging wholesale changes that would cost a lot of money, I have suggested certain modifications that would involve a better use of existing resources, and could therefore be actually described as economies. Furthermore, to stress that what we teach shall be useful rather than merely academic, is to invest language classes with greater pleasure and purpose, and to secure a better return on expenditure.

Far too long have the languages of the classroom been a kind of national joke, ranking with mothers-in-law, Civil Service tea, and the British climate. The music hall linguist, Mon-sewer Eddie Gray, symbolizes our frustration as well as our ignorance. The recordings of Hildegarde, with her

> Darling, je vous aime beaucoup;
> Je ne sais pas what to do,

would be even sillier than they are, if we ourselves were more efficient. Abroad, too, the tongue-tied Englishman afield than Broadstairs. Meet the people! urges a recent advertisement.[1] Wine with the workers of Paris! Dance with the dockers of Venice! Sing with the fishermen of the Adriatic! Today, these activities may be unattractive to the orthodox tourist; but if the 'common man' turns traveller, they will (unlike travel in first-class coaches, and residence in expensive hotels) call for a knowledge of languages.

What languages will be in use? Shall we, as I have suggested in the Foreword, have broken the French monopoly, or will it have been bolstered by some such scheme as *Le Monde Bilingue*, making French and English the principal foreign languages of every Western European country? Will it be Esperanto, or some latter-day equivalent? Whatever the media of communication that confront us in the second half of this century, language teaching will have to be on its mettle.

Many language teachers, I know, think that results fall far short of effort. Yet, mercifully, freedom is ours to experiment. If we do not use it, we shall remain mere technicians; our teaching will merely represent a way of earning money—and a dubious one at that—instead of an important and creative task.

[1] *New Statesman*, March 27, 1954.